do it for You

IAN ANDREWS

WORD PUBLISHING

WORD (UK) Ltd
Milton Keynes, England

WORD AUSTRALIA
Heathmont, Victoria, Australia

WORD COMMUNICATIONS LTD
Vancouver, B.C., Canada

STRUIK CHRISTIAN BOOKS (PTY) LTD
Maitland, South Africa

ALBY COMMERCIAL ENTERPRISES PTE LTD
Balmoral Road, Singapore

CHRISTIAN MARKETING NEW ZEALAND LTD
Havelock North, New Zealand

JENSCO LTD
Hong Kong

SALVATION BOOK CENTRE
Malaysia

GOD CAN DO IT FOR YOU

First published by Marshall Morgan & Scott 1982
This edition Word (UK) Ltd. 1990

ISBN 0–85009–344–9 (Australia 1–86258–089–8)

Reproduced, printed and bound in Great Britain for Word (UK) Ltd. by Cox and Wyman Ltd., Reading.

90 91 92 93 / 10 9 8 7 6 5 4 3 2 1

Contents

'But God forbid that I should glory,
save in the cross of the Lord Jesus Christ.'

Gal. 6.14

Thanks to all who have so willingly shared their personal experiences of God's steadfast love and faithfulness. Also to the one who patiently typed, and sometimes re-typed the stories, Mrs June Gollifer.

DEDICATED TO Rosemary, my wife and fellow worker in the Lord; also Stephen, my son, who has sacrificed so much family time for the sake of others.

Introduction

Ian Andrews is a Chartered Accountant by profession. He had a good position and bright prospects for the future. God began to work in his life while he was living in London and caused him to realise that there was someone and something missing. This someone was Jesus, who confronted him with the truth of his divinity and the reality of his teachings. Was God who he claimed to be? The hunger for a real experience with God grew until he made the decision to put his life and future into God's hands. This was the beginning of a new pathway which was to affect every area of his life.

It was wonderful to know God was hearing and answering his prayers in a practical way. God was becoming a reality. One day, after completing his office work, Ian sat down and opened his Bible at Ezekiel chapter thirty-nine – the fourteenth verse seemed to stand out from the page! 'And they shall sever out men of continual employment, passing through the land.' Three days later, he was made redundant.

It had always been relatively easy to find employment. This time, however, after applying for many positions and not being accepted, Ian began to question what God was saying to him. God always answers, and spoke to him, audibly this time, 'Go and preach the Gospel and heal the sick'. This presented a problem as Ian had suffered with a severe stammer for most of his life. His reply to God was, 'What me, Lord? I'd be thrilled to preach the Gospel and pray for the sick – only heal me first.'

But God's word is the last word. He said, 'No. You go as you are, then everyone will know who the Healer is, and that's *me* – I will heal you gradually as you go.' And that's what happened. For Ian, it was a humbling and sometimes frustrating experience, but he found that yielding to God is the best and only way to go.

To his surprise, and despite his own weakness and fears, God's life began to flow through him to heal people. It did not depend on Ian or how he felt. As people heard that Jesus took their pains and sicknesses on himself, they looked to God and were healed. One of the first people who came forward for prayer was a person who stammered as badly as Ian himself – and God healed him! Small sicknesses as well as severe diseases have been healed in the name of Jesus – nothing is too hard for the Lord.

As Ian's wife, I have known God's hand on our lives right from the start, but had no idea of the things God had in mind for us. It is an adventure to work together with God, and worth everything to follow Jesus. We love him because he first loved us and it is our desire that you know his fulfilment in your life too.

As you read these pages, you will know that Jesus is alive today. These are the true stories of just a few of the thousands who have been healed by God's power. They are told by ordinary people who have been touched by a wonderful God. Let hope and faith spring up in your heart as you read them, so you may know that God can do it for you!

Rosemary Andrews

I went hot all over

Mrs Grace Wilcox lives in Merseyside, North West England, with her husband and five daughters. After three years of almost total bed rest and one tragedy after another, the whole family is now full of praise to God for his goodness to them.

'It was December 1972 and a dark, cold evening, and life for our family was as dark and dismal as the winter outside. For some months Tony, my husband, had been out of work and the family had depended on my earnings as a presser in a factory making gas fires. With six children to feed and clothe it was all we could do to make ends meet. Then one day I grabbed the press handle as usual, pulled it down hard as I had done a thousand times before, and a searing, agonising pain shot through my back and left me clinging to the press handle and gasping with pain. It was out of the question for me to continue working. I couldn't move without crying out, so I was taken home where the doctor came to see me and told me I had sciatica. Like everybody else I had laughed about sciatica but not any more. For seven long weeks I lay on my bed scarcely able to move for the pain, and listening to the family sounds as Tony tried to cope with the kids. By the end of the seven weeks I was ready to scream with the frustration and pain and the clutter around me in our small, dilapidated house. Eventually the doctor sent me to the hospital and I was put on traction for a further four weeks with still no improvement. Finally I was taken to the operating theatre for a laminectomy which is the removal of a disc between the vertebrae. That helped a lot and I began to get back on my feet and was able to potter in the house.

'Then came that December evening. About five o'clock someone had to run to the shops before they closed and young Tony, our only son who was a sensible boy, offered to go. There was no reason why he shouldn't as he had so often before. But the time passed and he didn't return and then suddenly our lives crashed around us as we were told there had been an accident.

'The next hours were the darkest in our lives. Apparently when crossing the busy road young Tony realised something was coming, turned, and ran straight into another car. The nightmare of it all lived with us for years. God had taken our only son and we didn't know how to go on. If he was a God of love, how could he do this to us? In fact, was there a God at all and, if so, how could he be so cruel as to take away our only son? We were decent people. We had never harmed anyone. We went to mass regularly and did what the church told us to do. Where had we gone wrong? A deep bitterness welled up inside me as my thoughts went round and round in a state of resentment and rebellion. My husband reacted in a different way and perhaps the tragedy of that dark experience was really a turning point toward our eventual meeting with God.

'Walking home one evening soon after we lost Tony, my husband stopped and had a couple of beers to ease the sorrow in his heart, and then continued homewards along the street. As he passed a church he paused for a moment and cried out, 'God, you lost your Son and now I've lost mine. Please let Tom and Mary help us through life.' It was all spontaneous but God was listening. Tom is my brother and he and his wife Mary were terrific to us in our loss. They kept coming to visit and asking us to their house and in the end they encouraged us to move and make a new start in life. But Tony lost his job again and we were getting deeper and deeper in debt and there seemed to be no end to our troubles. Once in our new home we searched around and found a flat nearby for my mother and it seemed as if we were getting straightened out at last. Then tragedy struck again.

'It was a Sunday morning and Mary sent her boy, Paul, round to see his Granny as he did regularly at the weekend. But he came running back to say he couldn't get in and his Granny wouldn't answer the door. Mary called me and we went round together and found Mother dead in bed. She had been as fit as could be the day before. Again my reaction was one of deep bitterness and resentment.

'We were coping with this new loss when a letter came saying we owed so much rent money that, if we didn't do something about it, we would be turned out of our house. I can tell you, by this time the world and God seemed lined up against us and I really hated everybody. Then Tony got another job and I was able to go out to work again and things got a bit better. But all my life I've had trouble with overweight and this was when I decided to do something about it. The doctor gave me a diet which was something I found hard to cope with so, to help it along, I signed up for a 'Keep Fit' class. I began prancing around and flinging my arms about like the best of them and what did I do but put my back out again. Then followed a repeat performance of my previous back injury; eight weeks in bed, into hospital, four weeks traction, tests of all kinds, and then another operation to remove another disc. All the time this was going on questions and anger and depression and despair surged round and round inside me. Tony had managed to cope with the children because we had moved in to live with his father shortly before I injured myself this time. But money was short and Christmas was coming up so that, almost as soon as I was discharged from hospital, I took another job. Perhaps, at last, things were going to settle down. But no. As we began to gather bits and pieces for Christmas, so Pop, Tony's father, began having blinding headaches. They were so bad he couldn't stand us talking to him. Soon after Christmas he was taken into hospital where they diagnosed a cancer tumour and for three months we were up and down to visit him as they did one operation after another.

'Now I had a new list of questions going through my head. Why did this happen to Pop? He was such a good man. Why couldn't God let him die a decent death? Where had we all gone wrong? Of course it was all God's fault, I was convinced of that.

'Coming home after Pop's funeral the house seemed like a tomb. The girls were at school, young Tony had gone, Mother had gone, now Pop had gone. We needed money badly. There was no choice but for me to go back to my job and do what I could to help. That's what I did and for one week, only one week, everything went well. The second week I went up to the canteen and had no idea the floor had just been washed. Before I knew what was happening, I slipped, couldn't save myself and crashed onto my back. Struggling to my feet I somehow managed to get through the day. But the following morning I couldn't move. I couldn't bear it. Not again. 'God, I hate you. What are you doing to me?' But I was a prisoner again and followed the old routine. Two months in bed at home, into hospital, tests and tests and more tests. But, after three months tests no operation. The surgeon decided it was too dangerous and I might be paralysed for life. I was sent home to do my best and for a year only left the house every three weeks to go by ambulance for a check up. What ever it was I had done to myself my life seemed finished. When I dragged myself out of bed I was unable to straighten up but shuffled along bent double, my hands down by my feet. I was put in plaster for four months but it didn't help. When that came off I was given a plastic cast to wear but it was so uncomfortable I only wore it when I got up and then I couldn't stand the discomfort for long. My oldest daughter became nurse and mother and, still in her early teens, looked like being tied to the house for ever. It was no life for a girl at all. It was no life for any of us. Tony was near enough alcoholic; I was crippled in my mid-thirties. There was no point trying any longer. We were finished. Talking together one evening Tony and I decided the girls would have a better future without us. He was kneeling by my bed and beside us were all my tablets. The answer to our problems was staring us in the face. With no emotion we agreed that we would both take enough of my tablets to see us out of this world. But an extraordinary thing happened. We had no sooner made up our minds to do this when we both fell into a deep sleep. It could only have been God because on waking we never even thought of suicide again.

'One day about a week later, Tom and Mary called to see me because Tom said he had something special he wanted to tell me. Of all things he began to speak about finding Christ. He talked on and on about Christ coming into his life and making all the difference. It didn't mean a thing to me, in fact I thought he was going round the bend. But that wasn't all, he went on to say he had had a vision of me standing straight and that he believed God was going to heal me. Then I was sure he had gone nuts. People that I knew didn't go around having visions and there certainly wasn't any evidence I knew of that God was going to do something good to me. I'd given up on God long before and told Tom so. I heard him out and then told him to get lost and stop saying stupid things. But Tom didn't give up. He had had a real experience of God in his life some three months earlier and, when praying for Tony and me one night in that January of 1978 he suddenly found himself sobbing as if his heart would break. God had really met him and convinced him I was to be healed and he came right over to tell me. But, in my state of mind, how could I believe what he was saying? However, Tom was not to be put off and back he came week after week, sometimes twice in a week, to talk to me about Jesus. Gradually what he was saying got through to me and little by little I began to change. He was talking to Tony, too, and all the time he was praying for us both.

'Not long afterwards, in the same week in March, both Tony and I came to Christ, without each other knowing! I was lying in bed praying when I had a feeling of warmth inside me like a powerful light or a bush fire and tears started streaming down my face. Something was happening to me, something I had never experienced before. Somehow I knew it was Jesus and I found myself thanking him over and over again. With a feeling of peace I rolled over as I slept better on my tummy, but quite suddenly an extraordinary feeling filled me. It was as if my heart were suspended in a wind tunnel and the air was rushing through it and past it like a gale.

'Terrified, I rolled back and sat bolt upright, clutching my nightdress and not daring even to blink my eyes. But as I sat there shaking in the dark it was as if a gentle hand caressed me up and down my back and I heard a voice inside saying, 'Don't be afraid. It will be all right.' As quickly as it had gripped me the fear left and I was filled with such ecstasy, as if I was on the most fantastic holiday imaginable. The rest of the night I slept as I had never slept before.

'Waking next morning, far from finding it had all been a dream, I was still so high I knew I had been blessed by the Spirit of God. All I wanted to do was tell Tony and then Tom and Mary. And it was a Wednesday, the day Tom and Mary always came to visit me. So I shared with Tony what had happened to me and in the evening we sat, all excited, waiting for Tom and Mary to come. We waited and we waited. Eventually about eight o'clock we realised they were not coming. But I was ready to burst. Suddenly I had an idea.

' 'Let's go to them' I suggested to Tony. 'You call a taxi while I get into my 'armour'.'

' 'You can't get in a taxi in your state,' he objected. But my mind was made up and we went and what an evening we had! It was one o'clock in the morning before we stopped praising and praying and Tom ran us home in his car. All my questions and hatred and rebellion just vanished away when I met the real loving God. Now I felt I loved the Lord Jesus so much I didn't care if he wanted me to lie on my back for the rest of my life. And the wonderful thing was that Tony was also blessed in the Holy Spirit that same week and we were together in this.

'But Tom hadn't finished yet. He was thrilled that we had accepted Christ, but his vision went right on to physical healing for me as well. He prayed for me himself. He even invited his church prayer group to come and pray round me, convinced that if they only prayed hard enough I would get up and be healed! But most of them were busy and couldn't come and Tom was disappointed and upset that they didn't make the effort. But he was learning. Taking his disappoinment in prayer to God he was soon convinced that if God wanted me well he had the time and place already planned.

'Two months later, in May of 1978, Tom and Mary invited us to a meeting in Crosby Civic Hall. I nearly didn't go. I'd had to go out in the afternoon and when Tom and Mary came to fetch us the pain in my back was terrible. They walked in to find me sitting crying and so depressed I didn't even want to try and go out again. But they weren't taking no for an answer and Tom folded my wheelchair and put it in the boot without a word. When we reached the Hall he off loaded the chair and then picked me up bodily and carried me to it. Only then did Mary turn to me and say, 'You may be walking out of here tonight.' And that was the first I knew it was a healing meeting. If there was anything I needed that evening, it was healing. I felt terrible and I looked terrible. A friend of Tom's who saw us come in told us later I looked 'like death warmed up'.

'Once inside everything changed. The hassle of getting there was forgotten. People were singing and worshipping the Lord, and his presence was very very real. I was told the speaker was Ian Andrews and I wondered who he was. Coming from a Catholic background I was never quite sure about a Protestant speaker. But, when he began to speak I found I couldn't help but listen. Somehow the crucifix I had handled for years, and others I had looked at in churches, never came alive as did the story of the Cross that night. The crowds were forgotten as we were encouraged to use our imagination and picture what Jesus went through for our salvation and healing. For the very first time I forgot everyone around and saw Jesus as they strapped his hands above his head and got out the cat-o'-nine tails. Ian explained how that instrument of torture had lumps of lead or pieces of glass on the end of each lash and how it was lashed across the back of Jesus and drawn down, over and over again, tearing away the flesh and making the blood run.

'Ian went on to tell us that Jesus was not so concerned about the beating, but kept his thoughts on the reason for it. He told us he felt sure Jesus was looking forward to sitting alongside his Father in heaven, looking down on us and reminding his Father that every stripe he bore was to release us from sickness and make us well. 'God tells us in the Bible that we are healed by the stripes Jesus bore and Jesus longs for us to reach out and receive our healing by faith,' Ian explained.

'It was while we were being encouraged to see in our imagination what happened to Jesus that day, that Ian began to call out people with specific sicknesses. Suddenly I heard him say, 'There is a lady in the hall who has an injury to her spine and the Lord Jesus wants to heal her.' I knew that it was me, and at once felt all tingly with excitement and yet hot and bothered as well. Giving Tony a hefty nudge I said,

' 'That's me! Take me down! Take me down.'

'We were way up the steps near the back but I was so anxious to get to the front in case the offer closed, I suppose. And there wasn't a thing I could do.

'Suddenly both Tony and Tom rose to their feet together, grasped either side of my wheelchair and carried all seventeen stone of me plus my chair down the steps to the platform. And there we waited with me beseeching the Lord to bring Ian over to where I sat, and Tony and Tom standing like sentinels on either side of me.

'Meanwhile Ian had seen this procession and admitted later that he was scared. I looked so ill that it flashed into his thoughts that the morning paper would carry a headline, 'Minister Prays For Sick. Woman Dies!' But eventually there was no one but me left waiting and he came over to where I sat. Urging me not to do anything foolish unless I was certain I was healed, he told me to shut my eyes and he would pray for me. But I couldn't shut my eyes. I was so engrossed in visualising Jesus and all he did for me that, when Ian commanded my infirmity to leave and told me to be healed in the name of the Lord Jesus, I could see Jesus standing there, reaching out his hand to touch me.

'At first I thought I was going to die. My life seemed to drain out of me but then the Spirit of God came into me and a tremendous heat surged through me from the top of my head to the tips of my toes. I felt I went white hot all over. And then – I knew I was healed. I knew it, without a shadow of doubt. Fumbling to loosen the straps that held me in my chair, I stood up, took two or three steps and then sank on my knees praising the Lord. Ian thought his fears were realised and a St. John's Ambulance man came running from the back, but I knew I was healed. Scrambling to my feet and oblivious of anyone else, I shouted, 'Mary! Mary! Mary!' to tell my sister-in-law the impossible had happened. Ian thought I was praising the Virgin Mary and was confused, but nothing mattered at that moment because Jesus had come and Jesus had healed me and nothing was going to be the same ever again.

'Turning to give Tony a great big hug, there he was on the floor with tears streaming down his face and totally unaware of what had happened to me. He, too, had seen a vision of Jesus with his face surrounded by flames and a crown of thorns on his head and he was completely overcome.

'The rest of that evening was out of this world. We made our way home singing, 'Jesus loves me,' and other songs we had learned as children, and everything seemed marvellous until we reached home. I had gone out with my wheelchair a sick woman, I returned on my feet and full of excitement and joy. Bursting into the house, I expected my daughter to be as thrilled as I was but, instead, she gave one look and then turned right against me. It was some time later, when she herself came to Jesus, that she admitted she thought I had been conning her all those years to make her do all the work! Then I rang my sister, mind you it was the middle of the night by then. As soon as I heard her voice I said, 'Joan, I'm healed. The Lord Jesus Christ has healed me.' But, instead of joy, she couldn't believe what I was saying and told me, 'For goodness sake go to bed – you're drunk,' and hung up on me! Well, the disciples were told they were drunk, too, and we were delighted to be like them. After that I ran down our road knocking on neighbours' doors at one o'clock in the morning and saying, 'Look what the Lord has done for me.' But they thought I was mad so it seemed time to go to bed! And what a joy that was. For the first time for about three years Tony and I climbed the stairs, got in to bed together, and then lay for hours in each others arms praising the Lord and reliving all that had happened.

'When it came time for my hospital visit I was all excited. I walked in and immediately one of the nurses said, 'What ever has happened to you?' 'The Lord Jesus Christ healed me,' I told her. Then I saw the Registrar and he asked the same question. 'The Lord healed me.' 'The Lord who?' the poor man asked. 'The Lord Jesus Christ, of course,' I answered and he gave a little grin as if I needed psychoanalysing. Then he offered to sign me off as

I looked healthy enough but I wanted to see the Orthopaedic Surgeon who had tried his best to help me. In his busy schedule he made time to see me and out came the question. 'What happened to you?' When I told him, he commented that I looked absolutely marvellous, but then he asked if I had been to one of those fellows who stick pins in you. 'No,' I told him, 'I went to the greatest Physician of all, the Lord Jesus Christ.'

God keeps His promises

Rev. G. Paul Musselman in his mid eighties, carries a full load of ministry as Priest Associate of St. James Church, Ormond Beach, Florida. He was Director of the Central Department of Evangelism of the National Council of Churches 1960-61 and prior to that Director of the Division of Industrial and Urban Church Work for the National Council of the Episcopal Church with headquarters in New York City. Since receiving the Lord's healing touch, he and his wife, a former Catholic Bible Teacher, conduct a ministry based on healing.

'One Sunday evening in the late Fall of 1976, my daughter, helped by a kindly member of our Episcopal parish, tugged me to a Lutheran church where special healing services were being held. I was in no mood to accept anything anyone had to say about healing having lost my wife of more than half a century after her passing through years of suffering. I was next on the list for burial. As a matter of fact my own tombstone was erected at the time my wife's stone was put into the ground. My health had improved a little recently but it seemed to me to be a sort of cat and mouse game with death. However, I went with my daughter that evening and we sat in the next to back pew, far out of sight of whatever was going on up around the altar and pulpit area. The back pew was occupied by Episcopal laity and clergy who, like me, were determined to have a clear path of escape in case anything unseemly started going on.

'So we got settled and listened. What I heard was a subdued, smooth and rather resonant voice talking in a matter of fact way. Parson-like I immediately set to the task of analysing what the speaker had to say. Then suddenly he stopped and after a moment of hesitation announced, 'An elderly gentleman at the back of that section of the church has a serious heart condition.' I must admit I honestly missed the meaning of what he was saying and it certainly didn't occur to me that he was talking about me. He went on, 'There's another person at the back of the church with sinus trouble and allergies and asthma.' That didn't impress me at all for, as I whispered to my daughter, 'This is New Jersey, and who doesn't have the sniffles?'

'As no one moved, Ian Andrews, for it was he who was speaking, continued with his message and I realised he was giving biblically based teaching on God's care for people down through the centuries. He began at Exodus 15 where God told Moses to throw a tree into the bitter water that was undrinkable out in the desert and it became sweet. And he explained how this was a picture of applying the crucifixion of Christ that was to take place so long afterwards. God told the people in the desert that if they would obey him he would keep them from sickness. He even gave them one of his great covenant names, *Jehovah Rapha*, I am the Lord your Healer. This was very interesting and I forgot about the interruption over the man with the heart complaint. On the same theme Ian then moved on to Numbers 21 where the people of Israel, still in the desert, had been bitten by vicious little poisonous snakes and were dying like flies. Ian again showed how God answered prayer by telling Moses to make a snake like the one causing the trouble and set it up on a pole where everyone could see it. Those who looked in faith and went on looking, were healed and recovered no matter how near death they had been. This, too, Ian told the congregation that night, was a picture of Jesus being nailed to the Cross and held up for any who would look to be freed from their sin. Then, I remember, he went on to speak very movingly about the total sacrifice of Jesus

Christ, from the Garden of Gethsemane to the whipping post where he bore our sicknesses to the cross where he took the punishment for our sin.

'One or two other people began to go forward as the service was drawing to a close and it was then that a Catholic kid in the pew in front of me turned and, pointing his finger straight at me said,

''Chicken. It was you he was talking about!' So I had no choice. My daughter took me forward and I went reluctantly, clutching my bottle of white pills for angina in my hand. I think Ian was rather annoyed with me. He told me that I should have come up when God revealed my need and that I had nearly ruined the service. But then he asked if he could pray with me as he knew God wanted to heal me. He prayed and to my amazement I went down on the floor in what I like to call 'reclining worship'! But while I was on the floor the Spirit of God performed a mighty miracle in me. My doctor couldn't believe it when I later went to see him. Supernaturally God had implanted a double bypass coronary artery complete with a valve and given me a heart of a man of forty. I felt different at once but a little stunned and began to make my way back to my seat. On the way a little girl in a wheelchair reached out and took my bottle of pills out of my hand.

'You'll never need these again, Rev.!' she said, and praise the Lord she was absolutely right. What a lot I had to think about after that experience.

When my ministry began back in 1925 my duties included that of being Protestant Chaplain for a large city hospital and praying for the sick had always been a guarded and priority part of my priesthood. But somehow the prayers, though they carried the message of recovery, were seldom said with any deep belief in their effectiveness towards recovery. But something had happened to me when I was very ill with many diseases during the decade from the early sixties. This led me to reading systematically about what was going on in the Christian world and I found myself beginning to understand Ian Andrews as I learned about the growth of that extraordinary and ecclesiastically unplanned phenomenon known as Charismatic Renewal. I found that Ian Andrews was one of those men and women who spoke with complete assurance and whose faith was backed up by the Holy Spirit.

'After that evening, instead of heading for my engraved tombstone I seemed to be racing in precisely the opposite direction.

'At an unusual conference in Kansas City in 1977 which someone aptly called 'The Family Re-Union of the Christian Churches', I found myself waving my hands, singing in tongues, enjoying such uncharacteristic phrases as halleluia and praise the Lord, and singing Amazing Grace numerous times, off key but spiritually on the button. I participated in a Roman Catholic Mass celebrated by Cardinal Suenens when around thirty thousand Catholics sang in the Spirit and vested priests danced before the Lord. It was at that Mass that I told the Lord I would in future walk the King's highway, a commitment that had begun when the Lord through Ian Andrews had installed that by-pass artery to my heart.

'After that initial healing of my heart a lot of nasty conditions which gave me great pain began to get better rather than worse. One of these was emphysema. I was told that owing to my heart condition my lungs were nearly filled with stale blood and pain and near suffocation led to me screaming out in the night. But after that first touch from God I began to call the Oral Roberts Abundant Life Prayer Group in Tulsa several times a week and quite soon the lungs cleared. Then I went to a charismatic meeting in Plainfield and went forward for prayer for a miscellaneous lot of oozing ulcers all over various organs. I had also had pernicious anaemia but that all cleared.

'With all this in my history, my hard-pressed and very able physician suggested that my daughter and I move to

Florida where the climate would be easier for me. We settled in a beautiful but modest little one floor flat so popular here, which was easy for Polly to keep spick and span. I settled down with my adequate library, admired my easily kept lawn and got very popular with the neighbourhood kids as a pushover for cookies. But then my grey beard and the white hairs on my head gradually returned to their natural dark brown! I considered this too big a hint to be ignored so got busy again with the two most active Charismatic groups in the area both of which were operating in Roman Catholic churches.

'Late in October 1979, at a large Nuptial Eucharist in my own St. James Episcopal church, I became the husband of Dorothea Stemberger, who had been the first to bring to this area the news of the 'last revolution whereby Christ shall transform the world'. One of the features not provided for in the new Book of Common Prayer was that the Best Man fell out in the Spirit at the end of the service and then got up and shouted, 'I'm healed!' He had cracked five ribs waterskiing the previous day. The congregation, both Catholics and Episcopalians, applauded loudly!

'It was shortly after this that Ian Andrews called us up and first of all heard the news of the marriage of this supposedly dying priest to a Catholic widow with five children! Then he told us he was ready to come to visit us, had had an unexpected cancellation and could we take him at short notice? Could we? It was too late to get official sponsorship from church bodies and there was little enough time even to phone friends. But we set to work at once and it became a sort of whomsoever-will meeting in our house and God was on our side.

'Ian tackled the evening with little music and no real build up and the subject he spoke on was 'rejection', I have heard a lot of preachers circle some thorny patches without being badly scratched, but Ian waded right into this subject which, if you think about it, involves everybody and some people pretty nearly all the time. He did it in such a way that the next day I hurried to my library and found a whole new approach to group relationships from just the beginning of his talk.

'But he talked too long! No one became restless except my spiritually perceptive wife and myself but several others did rather think he was going on a bit. However, there was a reason and this reason tells something very vital about Ian Andrews and his finely tuned spiritual perception. He kept talking because he felt a demonic hostility. My wife felt it too and quietly reached out her hands and gathered a group of six or seven who prayed quietly. Then one man got up and left. And it was then that Ian moved on into healing, and the Holy Spirit was there to bless that night. Among many Catholics present there was the leader of a large group who had asked Mr. Andrew's permission to record the evening. Later he told us that when the tape was replayed there was interference of some kind for most of the recording. This suddenly stopped and the rest of the recording was clear. Careful timing afterwards proved that when the hostile person left the room the recording cleared.

'To finish I must share my own most fragrant memory of Ian Andrews' ministry. I was told that he was again visiting the New Jersey Lutheran church where I had received my heart healing. So I flew up there to hear him and found the church packed with many standing. Then a man vacated the end seat in a pew and I zeroed in for it. It was the only vacant seat to be seen and nobody moved towards it but me – so any latent convictions about selfishness were appeased. But I soon found out why that man had moved and I had taken his seat. It was God's plan for me to sit there. When I sat down, a little girl of about eleven or twelve years of age moved over her father's lap and sat next to me. She was shaking like a leaf in the wind and there was pain and pleading in her face. As we sat there I took both of her nervously twitching hands in mine and began to pray quietly. Then she pulled her left leg around and I saw the ghastly ugliness of the very worst club foot I have ever seen. Her father looked at me and then whispered that she also had no knee cartilage.

'When the message ended and Ian began to minister to the long line of expectant and needy people, I was so breathlessly interested in the wonderful healings and so busy praying for the little girl that I nearly missed getting into the healing line before it ended. But almost as Ian was finished, I picked up the little girl and walked across the sanctuary praying that Ian would stay long enough to pray for this poor little disfigured girl. Praise the Lord he did. He turned to her and said quietly, 'I don't think you like those shoes you are wearing.' She began to cry and said she hated them. Ian went on, 'Well, I don't think Jesus likes them any better than you do.' Then he gently invited her to sit on a chair and stretch out her legs towards a board he was holding. Then, in full view of the packed congregation who were watching in silence, he said to the little girl, 'Now watch Jesus get you ready for a new and nice pair of shoes.'

'And Jesus did!

'Immediately as everyone watched in utter silence, the club foot straightened out to match itself against her other foot on the board. Then there was an audible click and the knee jerked straight. The cartilage had come in! And up leaped the little girl and started jumping up and down and kicking her legs before diving at Ian and giving him a great big hug. Several dozen friends who had come with the girl, rushed up to thank God and his minister for that night's healing. God had once more brought to pass what he promised through the power, person, suffering and resurrection of Jesus Christ.'

God is so good

Stephen Dennis lives in Sussex, England, with his adoptive parents and sisters. He is always active, rebuilding chicken houses, planting potatoes, and cutting the grass. He has natural pitch and a lovely singing voice. His relationship with his sisters is that of a typical young brother, and his school progress is encouraging. To allow him to continue to fill in areas previously blank in his life, he has remained at a small school where he is not swallowed up in a huge class. His doctor sees him every six months to monitor his progress. His story is told by his adoptive mother.

'I was bored and feeling unfulfilled. My two lovely daughters had reached school age and, after seeing them on their way each morning, it was the same old routine day after day. It was all right for Ron, my husband, he was at work and occupied and came in in the evenings to enjoy his family but I had reached the point where the years stretched ahead in unrelieved sameness. When we were first married we had both thought we would one day have a son – we had even thought he would be called Stephen, but the girls had come and were now at school and I was wondering if this really was all life held for me. In fact one day my rebellion spilled over and I stood in the kitchen and declared to the empty walls, 'All I can do is wash dishes, change nappies, look after children, cook meals and clean the house.' It didn't help when I went to our church that same evening and someone spoke about Moses and the time when the Lord asked him, 'What have you got in your hand?' Moses held a rod and it became the rod of God but all I had was a dishcloth and I could see no way that God could use that.

'However, perhaps those walls were not as empty as I thought because soon after my little outburst Ron and I were talking and both felt we had love in our hearts for another child. This led us to consider fostering and soon we were going through the procedure of becoming foster parents.

'The following February, some time after we had been accepted, the phone rang and I can remember the feeling of excited apprehension when it turned out to be the authorities asking if we would take a four week old baby boy for two weeks. The fact that he was called Stephen didn't seem significant at the time, but it did seem quite a coincidence that his birthday was the same as that of our eldest daughter.

'For some reason I expected Stephen to be like any other baby but when he arrived I was shocked. He was dehydrated and wizened, far below his birth weight of a robust eleven pounds, and, worst of all, he appeared almost lifeless. He had bad septic areas under his arms and on his heels and his little bottom was bleeding and raw. I must say this was not what I had expected and I remember looking at this pathetic child and telling myself that somehow I was to love and care for this baby even though it would have to be through sheer willpower.

'The two weeks passed and the home situation not having been resolved, it became clear that Stephen was going to need fostering for a much longer period. That in itself was not a problem but, when we were accepted for the job, there had been an oversight in the paper work. Somehow it had been overlooked that we were obliged to sign two undertakings. The first presented no problem at all. It was that the child should be brought up as our own. But the second rocked us. We were asked to sign that we would encourage any child under our care in his or her own religion. Stephen's religious background was not the same as ours and we couldn't possibly sign that clause. We are Christians who know Jesus as our Saviour and Lord and it was out of the question that we should send Stephen off to a church on his own while we went elsewhere with the girls. How could we bring him up as our own and yet go in different directions over such an important matter? I felt physically sick as we considered the implications not only for Stephen but for any child that might come under our care.

'I rang the department dealing with our case and a social worker was sent along to see me. Fully expecting Stephen to be taken away and our names to be struck off the register, I tearfully explained our difficulty. It was extraordinary, but after only two weeks that pathetic little baby had crept into our hearts and we had come to love him in a very real way. But nothing very dramatic happened. The social worker spoke to the director in charge and, because Stephen was only a baby, the religious clause was waived until he was older, if he should still need a foster home.

'Weeks turned into months and still Stephen was with us. I started mixed feeding and watched as the lifeless little child began to improve. This encouraged us but at the same time other symptoms caused concern. For example, even a young baby will push with his feet and bounce on your lap. Stephen never did. And then at seven months he began losing weight rapidly and by ten months had to be admitted to hospital for dietary investigation. While in hospital other tests were carried out to see if his hearing was normal because he never said, 'Mum' or 'Dad' or turned his head when we spoke. These hearing tests proved negative as did others for autism. The only normal reaction Stephen showed at this stage was that he would laugh if he was tickled.

'Then we had a real blow. Although Stephen's mother had only visited him once at our home and seemed happy about the situation, I had to go into hospital myself for treatment and the wheels began to turn to find other foster parents for Stephen. With sad hearts we began to pray that only the best for Stephen should take place. It was a hard time for all of us. Our hopes were raised as one family decided against taking him, but then another offered. Then they changed their minds, but a third couple, older people, then wanted him and were able to sign the religious clause.

'By this time we were both home again and my spirits were at their lowest. Arrangements were made for me to take Stephen to visit this last couple and, although I prayed for strength, my heart was broken. The girls and Ron were as upset as I was. We felt as if our family was being broken in two.

'One morning Ron was reading his Bible and praying about the situation, when a verse in the second Psalm seemed to leap from the page. 'Thou art my son, this day I have begotten thee.' He knew the verse referred to Jesus, God's Son, but the way it had been drawn to his attention assured him God was telling him something. He read on, 'I will give you the heathen for your inheritance,' and he knew in his heart it was all going to turn out all right with regard to Stephen.

'Poor Ron, he tried to tell me what had happened and what he believed God was saying, but I never heard a word. I was so wrapped up in my negative thoughts that it ran off like water off a duck's back. But God is so good. That same evening Ron stayed with the children while I went to a fellowship at our church. The way I felt that evening, I opened up and told all my friends the calamity that lay ahead. Several prayed about Stephen and his future, but one man who prayed came over to me afterwards and said, 'I don't know if it means anything to you, but the Lord brought a verse to me from Psalm 2. 'Thou art my son, this day I have begotten thee.' Believe me, I was in such a state that I didn't realise it was the same verse Ron had been given that morning. It wasn't until I got home and told him what had happened that I came to believe everything was under God's control and would turn out all right.

'Even then my stomach did a flip when I saw the social worker coming to our house a few days later. But she brought good news. Stephen's mother had signed a paper giving us freedom to bring Stephen up in our faith! One hurdle was behind us and we were full of thanksgiving.

'It was not until Stephen was two years old that the doctors diagnosed a rare condition called galactosaemia which is when two enzymes are missing in the liver. The patient is allergic to all milk products and man-made foods such as sausages, baked beans, ice cream, sweets, in fact most of the things children enjoy. But this had gone on so long undiagnosed through Stephen's general debility that we were told irreversible brain damage had been done. However, he was put on a very strict diet and the change that made was incredible. Within three weeks he recognised us, called us 'Mum' and 'Dad', responded to Ron when he came in from work and, perhaps best of all, the constant diarrhoea he had had from the time he came to us, cleared up. It was a vast change but he was still floppy and had no muscle tone. But it was a big step forward.

'While all this was going on we were going through a time of considerable conflict in another way. I had been sick and God had healed me. Friends of ours had been sick and God had healed them. We were unshakably sure that God is a healer and one of his names is, 'The Lord, your healer.' Then why not Stephen? Why should God leave him in such a physical, mental and emotional mess if he was the healer?: I must confess I became quite bitter at times. We fasted, we prayed, we got together with friends and all 'agreed together', and Stephen stayed the same or even got worse. Then one evening I went to a prayer meeting and someone got up and said we ought to praise God for everything, no matter what. That was too much. I burst out in anger, 'Do you mean to tell me I have to thank God that Stephen is mentally retarded, that he's a physical wreck, that he can't bear his weight on his legs and may never grow into a mature adult?' In the silence that followed my outburst the man who had spoken gently suggested I should try to release Stephen to God and thank him anyway. I just sat and wept. What did he know about our kind of problem anyway? I could agree that we should thank God for normal ups and downs of life, but for Stephen's condition? How could I?

'The battle raged in my thoughts for the rest of the evening but, in the end sheer logic won out. We had tried everything and nothing had really helped so, if God is who he says he is and knows all things, maybe I should praise him and let him do what he was wanting to do in Stephen's life. Right at the end of that evening I was able to pray, 'God, I don't understand what you are doing but thank you that things are the way they are. I ask you to give me the grace to walk in gratitude before you even if Stephen is never healed.'

'Some people would call it coincidence but from that time there were many changes in Stephen's condition. He started to walk, he got a semblance of toilet training, he even began to feed himself, very messily, but he managed. Soon he began to sing and could pick up a tune quite well. But, with all these changes for the better, an ugly new symptom reared its head. He began to have uncontrollable temper tantrums and show an aggression we had not seen before. Yes, he could walk now, but that meant he wouldn't stay in bed at night and, when we tried to restrain him, he flared up in a rage. Our nights were disastrous. Stephen slept a mere four to five hours and during his sleep wet his bed twice at least, each night. Added to all this, on one of his hospital checks he was discovered to have a pronounced heart murmur.

'It just had to be God that led us to apply for adoption when Stephen was five and it became clear that his mother would not be able to care for him. We were warned that years of problems lay ahead if we went ahead with the idea, but it was the magnitude of Stephen's problems that convinced us he desperately needed a life commitment.

'About that time he began school but was so slow he only went in the mornings. With seventy-five children in one room and only two teachers Stephen decided not to stay and so he walked out and did it so often he was made to wear two green bands so that he could be found more easily. In spite of being allocated a welfare worker to stay beside him in school, it proved so impossible that he had to be withdrawn after only two terms. By now he was like a tornado physically and the afternoons were spent up on the Downs running off his energy to prevent him wrecking the home.

'Eventually, Stephen was admitted to Great Ormond Street Childrens' Hospital to try to sort out his problems, but even there he put his arm through a window and went missing alone in London.

'It was while he was in Great Ormond Street that I went to a meeting at Burgess Hill and again Stephen was prayed for. I went up to the hospital the next day and was told that they couldn't understand why but the day's tests were all negative whereas previously they had been positive. They could only suggest that I took Stephen home, took him off his diet and waited to see what happened. The specialist spoke to me when Stephen was discharged and he said, 'I'm not so worried about his diet, it's his behaviour that bothers me. He's going to need special help.'

'On our return Stephen was sent to the diagnostic unit of a special school, his behaviour problem being, if anything, worse than ever. But God is so good. At this new school we found Stephen's teacher was a dedicated Christian with a clear vision of a child's place in the world and an insight into children's problems. With her help he began to make slow progress but one day she underlined my fears by saying, 'You know, Stephen has big problems. He will grow up to be a thug but I'm glad he's with a Christian family. I dread to think what his future will be.' She really put my fears into words because he was so violent by now that he terrorised any baby sitter and we realised it was impossible to go out together. By this time he had developed asthma, had severe eczema and the murmur in his heart was becoming a problem.

'Stephen was seven when we were finally cleared for adoption and it was about that time that I had an experience with him that really frightened me. I was in the kitchen when I heard a crash and ran through to find that he had knocked a pot over and there was soil all over the place. I fetched the brush and dust pan and was sweeping up the mess when suddenly he came at me, kicking out viciously at my head. I had to defend myself with the brush and dust pan. It didn't last long but afterwards my heart was beating fast and I was frightened of what he might do next. I don't know why, but I had thought for some illogical reason, that once Stephen was legally ours everything would sort itself out and things would improve. Instead, by the time the adoption was through I felt thoroughly battered both physically and spiritually. The strong love that had grown in me for this child was unexpectedly damaged and I felt I couldn't trust him. My friend's prayers steadied me and helped me commit the situation to God, but I had an unease I hadn't known before.

'And then, right at that time of uncertainty we heard there was to be a meeting at Hove Town Hall and Ian Andrews was coming for a healing service. Ron and I talked it over together and decided we would go and take Stephen. After all, everybody had tried all they knew to help him with no real success so we were out on a limb before God. So many times he had shown he cared about Stephen, dare we hope that he might lovingly touch our boy and change his entire future?

'Arriving at the Town Hall we found the place almost filled but there were two seats near the front, right in the middle of a row. Ron was playing the organ that night so he was alright so Stephen and I pushed our way in and I settled down with a sense of expectancy. We prayed there might be a word from God through Ian for Stephen – a word of knowledge describing his condition. But, no, that didn't come. And yet, in a way, the message Ian gave that night was our answer. He was speaking about the blood that Jesus shed for us and explained that everywhere the blood of Jesus was spilled it was to reconcile us to God. And then he went into this more deeply and showed us that when Jesus went aside to pray in the garden of Gethsemane, the Bible tells us he sweat great drops of blood. Ian explained that when Jesus sweat those drops of blood he redeemed us from the curse in Genesis three verse nineteen: 'In the sweat of thy brow shalt thou eat bread.' Man had sinned and incurred the curse of God and God declared that as a result man would live by tension, by emotional stress, by mental problems, all the days of his life. In Gethsemane, Jesus came under such emotional and mental stress that something broke and he actually sweat, physically, drops of blood on his forehead. Ian shared with us that night that God had shown him this occurred to heal us of mental and emotional problems and even of retardation, spasticity and anything wrong with the brain.

'At the close of the meeting we were determined to reach Ian with Stephen so that he could receive whatever God had for him. This was anything but easy as the Town Hall was packed and we were well and truly hemmed in. But we eventually reached the front just before eleven o'clock when people were clearing up and beginning to go home. Ian asked us what we were wanting from God. What could we say? There was so much. We told him of the galactosaemia and aggression and lack of response to God, but whatever we said, God also spoke to Ian, telling him that Stephen's rejection as a baby had been so severe as to leave him as a spiritual orphan – a person with no security. So he prayed against an orphan spirit but then went on to pray that Stephen should be spiritually born again. Up to that time Stephen had shown no interest in the things of God but Ian told us later that God had shown him that, deep within, there was an interest and even a desire. That was all. We had done what we set out to do and we went home in cold faith.

'The next morning, as we wondered if anything would be different so soon, Stephen came happily downstairs having fully dressed himself for the first time in his life. He tapped his chest and said with a smile, 'I've got Jesus living inside me now.' He knew something dramatic had happened to him. He was still full of energy but the aggression had gone and there was a new quietness in his spirit. I was busy getting breakfast for the family when I thought I heard something. It was Stephen singing! He was singing the scripture songs he had appeared not to hear when we took him to church. That settled it for me. I knew God had done something very special and very wonderful. And that was probably what decided me to take some giant steps of faith and see what happened. First it was the asthma inhaler. That was left on one side and later put away never to be used again. Then, at bed time, Stephen had a real bath with real soap, something I had never used for six or seven years on account of the eczema. But that first day was full of new things. Stephen even picked up a piece of paper and wrote on it 'Stephen Dennis' as if he had been doing it all his life. I can tell you I had a lump in my throat and joy in my heart as the impact of what God had done in Stephen became clearer.

'Once back at school it was normal school dinners – with no bad reactions, and, like other children, Stephen copied off the board and did his sums, getting them right instead of refusing to even try and do them. But most noticeable of all, that awful aggression had gone and fights and visits to the headmaster to be reprimanded were things of the past.

'Eventually the day came for his hospital appointment. I had a few butterflies about going because the doctor had earlier advised us to save ourselves a lot of worry by putting Stephen into a childrens' home. As it was we were taken in to see another doctor and the visit was quite humorous. He went through Stephen's notes carefully, stopping to ask me questions as he read.

'What about the bed wetting?'

'That has stopped completely.'

'And the diet?'

'I've taken him off that.'

'Now. Stephen's asthma.'

'He no longer needs the inhaler.'

'Well, what about the eczema?'

'There isn't a trace of eczema left.'

'Eventually he asked me what had happened and I simply told him Stephen had been prayed for and God had healed him. With such a change in Stephen, he then got quite enthusiastic and told Stephen to run round the room and then jump on and off a chair before listening for the troublesome heart murmur. There was no murmur. Finally when I told him the frightening aggression had also gone, he looked at me and said,

'Well, we could do nothing and something had to be done by somebody.'

'Today Stephen is a new person, busy asking questions and learning about the things that interest boys. He is car-oriented and knows the owners of cars of certain makes living near his home. He wants to know where babies come from and spends time building 'Leggo'. There has been no more eczema, asthma or heart murmur and he loves to play football. God has done so much for Stephen and we firmly believe he will complete what he has begun. We hoped he would catch up with others boys of his age but he is slower at reading and writing than average. He also needs to be careful what he eats as there is still a tendency to stomach pain if he takes milk products or highly-flavoured foods. But God has performed miracles in Stephen's life and God is alive and Love-incarnate and we can believe him to continue his work in Stephen even as he is doing in us.'

The vision of a piece of liver

Mrs. Vanje Kempster is a model and speaker at Christian Women's Clubs in Canada and the United States. She and her lawyer husband, Brian, live with their family in Ontario, Canada.

Vanje was determined not to cry. After only five weeks of married life, here she was seeing her husband off to the north of Canada on a job that would last five months. Somehow her dreams were shattered before they had hardly formed. At nineteen she had been so thrilled to promise herself in marriage to a law student, but a law student that was different. Brian Kempster had life and determination and talent and it was all so glamorous and exciting to his young sweetheart. He had been a night club entertainer, but also had a head on his shoulders which landed him a job as a male secretary with a railway company which held out prospects of rapid advancement to the top. He carried this job together with his night club circuit. But things had gone wrong. Not one but two of his friends had become alcoholic and Brian had done a rethink about his future as a result. He had no intention of following in his friends' footsteps and wasting his life. He decided to get out of the night club world while the going was good and settled down to study for a university degree in law. However marriage to Vanje was on the programme so they went ahead with their plans, she moved from the country to the city and they bought themselves a mobile home. But Brian was not satisfied with scraping his way through his course on a pittance. All along he wanted success and that meant enough finances to more than get by. Then a summer job came up that was going to ease any financial burden and so, after a mere five weeks together, the mobile home was let to summer students and Vanje returned home to live with her parents. But she was not going to cry.

Crying had been part and parcel of those first hectic weeks and Brian, older and with more experience of life, had been annoyed. He couldn't understand what it was all about. He was aiming straight for the top and now he had married a young girl who did nothing but cry.

So at nineteen, Vanje returned home with a problem. It was a mistake of course, she knew at once, because she was no longer her parents' child but a married woman and yet she had had so little experience and such a short time to adjust to married life that she wasn't sure whether she really was child or woman.

If her parents didn't understand her and her husband wasn't there to try to help her into adulthood, at least her friends did their best. Vanje was included in all they did which meant she was involved in a seemingly endless round of parties. And when none of them was giving a party, who was the perfect person to arrange one but Vanje, the lonely young wife? Far from sitting at home moping, Vanje's life became a ceaseless round of hectic activity. With all the energy of youth she held down a job, threw herself into night life without getting her proper rest, and was quite certain, as young people are, that nothing could go wrong with her. But Vanje was playing about with something lethal that she didn't understand. All her friends involved her, which was very commendable, but the way of life of her friends centred around drink. Drinks to welcome you, drinks to loosen your tongue, drinks to say farewell. And when Vanje was not with one friend she was with another and as they all lived on the same formula, Vanje was drinking with each and all of them and that meant she was drinking more than any of them. What's more this inexperienced young bride liked her drinks straight and often and it was not long before she made excuses to stay on overtime at work so that she could drink on her own with no one around to complain.

In the Fall, Brian returned from the north to do the next seven or eight months in school and they moved back into their mobile home to carry on life together. But Brian's determination to succeed had not lessened one bit and every night he took himself off to the law library to continue his studies while Vanje stayed on her own in their little home. Of course the tears started again and Brian was upset but this time Vanje didn't worry too much about the effect of her tears on her husband. By now her friends were an important part of her life and it was her friends she wanted to impress. Vanje wanted to be thought courageous and mature and able to handle life as it was coming to her so she crushed her hurts deep within and built a hardness inside to protect herself.

That was when she became ill. For no reason she could think of, everything she ate – or drank – came straight back up again. Speaking of those days she says,

'It was terrible. From the word go our marriage was beset with problems. And now, after five months away, Brian returned to a young wife he scarcely knew only to have her jumping out of bed night after night to throw up.' And things got worse. Even a glass of water came back and any weight this slim young woman carried, fell away leaving her thin and haggard and obviously very ill. Her condition became so serious she was hospitalized and put through every test applicable and the diagnosis returned was hepatitis. But with diet and care and words of advice, Vanje eventually returned home and everything seemed back to normal.

The next summer Brian went up north for another five months and the whole business began again. In fact Vanje almost felt a sense of release to return to her friends in a more full way once her husband had left her on her own. Almost immediately her troubles began. Her friends whom she dearly loved were either separated, divorced or living common law and, to drown their own problems, heavy drinking had become their way of life. Once back among them with all barriers down, Vanje reverted to their way of life and picked up the threads of disaster. In fact, by the time Brian returned the next time it was a problem for her to give up her constant companionship with her friends and return to the restrictions of married life.

That year Vanje became really ill. The hepatitis flared up again, she was hospitalized and this time it was serious. She says,

'I knew I was in a bad way and I was scared. People came to see me who had never been near me before and this convinced me I was either dying or close to death.'

To make matters worse this young woman, barely in her twenties, shared a small room with a terminal cancer case. Vanje put two and two together and decided the doctors considered her to be a terminal case also. Why else would they be together? Lying there, feeling so deathly ill, she listened as the other poor woman prayed and prayed. But that wasn't Vanje's style at all. In fact, when the poor dying woman tried to tell Vanje about the love of Jesus, Vanje dismissed the subject on the grounds that her companion must be mentally affected. The endless tests of the previous year were repeated and this time her sickness was diagnosed as 'infectious hepatitis.'

Plenty of rest and a variety of medication once more eased Vanje's condition and she was sent home to start life over again.

By this time Brian's studies were completed, he had qualified and he was on the look out for that job that would lead to fame and fortune, particularly fortune. Vanje had begun a modelling career and a man in Fredericton was putting together a photographic portfolio for her. Things seemed brighter than they had been for a long while. However, marriage is primarily to the end of producing children and this was the time when they agreed to begin a family. And of course, becoming pregnant put an end to Vanje's modelling career just as it was getting off the ground. It all seemed so unfair to her. Why did she have to be the one who gave up everything? Her early years of marriage had turned out to be a lonely, sickness-riddled vigil. Now, with her own ambitions falling around her a resentment grew and grew in her spirit and eventually bore its own ugly fruits. Vanje developed a severe, persistent skin allergy that was to remain with her for many years. To cap everything Brian found that job with prospects he was looking for but it was far away in Ontario. This time it was five weeks after their first son was born that he left Vanje once again and she had to make the best of things until she and her baby could join him and set up home together in a totally new area.

So began an extraordinary way of life. Living in a small community Brian and Vanje threw themselves into a whirl of social life that they enjoyed and believed to be necessary to make their way in the world. They joined the right clubs, played golf with the right people, went to parties whenever possible, always, of course turned out to perfection with Vanje in a new dress for each occasion – you couldn't be seen dead in the same dress twice. And with all these functions there were the drinks. When it was their turn to hold a party no one considered tea or coffee, never mind tonic water! It had to be the real thing and plenty of it whether it was for a private dinner party or an all-out affair with a hundred and more present.

That was the life the world saw, accepted and admired. When the doors were closed it was a different story. Behind the scenes for the next ten years life was to be dominated by diets, creams, lotions, plastic gloves, persistent vomiting and endless, gnawing, debilitating pain, 'as if someone were digging a finger deeply into me under my ribs,' Vanje describes it. Even caring for her conservatory caused problems because Vanje's allergies multiplied until every kind of dust brought out her skin lesions, and tending the plants in the conservatory was lethal. Night after night she lay beside Brian scratching, scratching until her hands were bleeding and Vanje was sobbing it hurt so much.

Then through the summer of 1972 something quite unexpected happened in the town where the Kempsters lived. For eight to ten days a local church gathered people from all denominations and no denominations and the Spirit of God moved in that church. It was a church that believed in the inspiration of scripture, and believed in the need for conversion, but in its history had never experienced a full measure of revival fires! The evangelist who came was not much as preachers go, but God came down on the people with a spirit of real repentance and, night after night, the church was packed.

And Brian and Vanje? They were at their lodge in the north safely tucked away from all that God was doing and about as far in the world as it was possible to be. Except that, unknown to Vanje, Brian had been aware of the call of God to follow him for several years. Of course it was out of the question. How could he be successful if they withdrew from their way of life and in particular put a stop to their social drinking? But when God calls he wants an answer and in his love he will engineer a way of putting forward his demands in a way that cannot be ignored. Somehow, that September, Brian and Vanje were persuaded to attend a Christian conference together and this was God's time to put forward his claim on their lives.

Sitting down to the very first meal, they looked around at some eight hundred delegates and felt unknown and like fish out of water. But God never fluffs his plans and sitting at the table with them was the right man at the right time to make the impact on them that they needed. This man's life was a carbon copy of Brian's life! Every instance he shared Brian could relate to exactly and Vanje also as the one who had been part of his life. As they listened to what could have been their own story, they heard how

Jesus had been first held at bay, then allowed to come in and take over and of the transformation that had taken place in this man's life as a result. By the time his story ended Brian had been brought face to face with the fact that their life-style was keeping them from an encounter with God.

'We committed our lives totally to God and were convicted by him to start a whole new way of life.'

This was God's plan, not theirs. Certainly nothing had been further from Vanje's thoughts. But the power of Jesus touched their lives at that conference and turned their hearts to God.

So! How to start? Heading for home in the car they came to a joint conclusion. Drinking was finished, and that had to be supernatural. It had to be God.

'I was drinking a lot of wine at the time and in terrible pain and deathly ill after every drink,' Vanje admits. 'But when we declared ourselves for Christ the first thing that came to me was that I must stop drinking.' Knowing this was going to be a turning point in their lives, for a moment she entertained the idea of explaining the change on medical grounds but, driving back together in the car, Brian decided to come clean and cease serving drinks from that time on and Vanje agreed fully.

'It took three months for everyone to cross us off their list and put an end to all our social friends and activities!' Vanje tells. 'I often wonder if they were afraid of the fact we were Christians or if they just didn't know what to do with us.' Whatever the reasons, they were certainly at the receiving end of a lot of gossip and speculation. Pressures and problems rained in on them, but they know now that it was permitted by God as his way of shaping them for his service. He had work for them to do for his glory and there was a lot of remoulding of their lives and characters needed before they could be used to the extent he had in his plan.

But Vanje was still sick. Nothing had changed in that way. Spiritually she was new and fresh and eager to learn, but physically it was the same old story of sickness, allergies, pain and pills. But no loneliness. Yes, their old friends had cut them off, but, whereas the house had been filled for parties, now these two new people opened it for Bible study and prayer. And, to their joyful astonishment the new look gatherings took off at once and grew and grew. The first night sixty turned up, then seventy, then eighty. And this for Bible study and prayer! Soon they were inviting men of God to come and teach and share with them. There was a whole new richness and hunger in the meetings that kept them alert to those who were available in the Christian world.

One of their speakers, Walter Day, came from England and he suggested Brian and Vanje should invite a friend of his, Ian Andrews, to speak to them. That was fine and Ian was booked to come for several days but, somehow, when he arrived he didn't seem to be quite the same as their previous visiting speakers.

Brian took him into the living-room and was seeking to make him feel at home when Ian announced,

'I had a vision on the plane coming here.'

Thinking he meant a vision in his spirit of blessing for the visit, Brian encouraged him to say more.

'It was a vision of a diseased, decomposing piece of liver,' Ian told him. With someone other than Brian that could have ended not only the conversation but even the visit. But Brian had had such an experience of God in his life that he not only accepted Ian's extraordinary statement, but immediately associated it with Vanje's condition. At the time, however, he simply asked Ian how the vision should be interpreted.

'I am going to meet someone here who is alcoholic and whose body is suffering from abuse by drink,' Ian said quietly. 'I believe God has given me the vision because he intends to heal someone in that condition.' Brian, wondering at his apparent boldness, asked Ian how he could be so sure and Ian told him that on other occasions he had been given a vision before taking a series of meetings and in each similar case the vision had been fulfilled by a healing

Brian waited eagerly for Vanje to be healed, but Vanje, dramatic as ever, waited all week for some poor alcoholic to walk in the door, come to Christ and be healed. It had never occurred to her that although she was not an alcoholic, the use of alcohol had severely aggravated her condition and she was the one who was going to be touched.

However, one day as they were sitting talking together, Ian described in detail the vision and the condition of the person to whom it applied. It was so clearly her own physical state that Vanje became nervous inside and at last asked the Lord if she could be the one to whom Ian was referring. She was so grateful that Ian had allowed God to convince her and had not imposed his interpretation of the vision on her. But she still hid from him the possibility that she could be the one, and also hid the other physical condition that had troubled her for the past eleven years or so.

The meetings continued night after night but about midweek when Vanje went to the study to fetch Ian, he looked at her, crossed the room slowly and said, 'Vanje, you are the one with the liver condition.' Then he paused for a moment before adding, 'What's more you have another physical problem, don't you? God is going to deal with that as well and he is going to heal you this evening.'

'I was so awed and nervous I couldn't say a thing,' Vanje admits. 'I couldn't believe something was going to happen to me, and yet I didn't want to miss what God had planned for me. I was scared and excited at the same time if you know what I mean.

'You can imagine how I felt. People were pouring into our house and filling up the chairs and there was I feeling detached and apprehensive and very excited. I could scarcely greet people as they came in and in the end found myself a space on the floor where I couldn't be seen!

'It was a tremendous and wonderful evening. At first I had trouble controlling my thoughts but as he went on, Ian's talk gripped my attention. He read about the wedding in Cana from St. John chapter two and the first thing he said really thrilled me. That Jesus began his ministry at a wedding and he would finish it at a wedding, his own, the marriage supper of the Lamb. Then, talking of turning the water into wine, he spoke of God's desire to turn our natural, flat rather ordinary lives into something sparkling, thirst-quenching, full bodied and effervescent. Something tremendous and supernatural.'

But for the expensive carpet, you could have heard a pin drop. Everyone present was drinking in all Ian was saying and getting caught up in the presence of the Lord that filled the room. He went on to say how God wants us as Christians, to enjoy a supernatural life-flow. Then, speaking of the fact that the best wine came at the end of the wedding, Ian assured his listeners that, in these last days, God is going to do something that will really satisfy our hearts.

'Quite simply,' Vanje relates, 'I can only say that God then began to do wonderful things in our room. One dear older lady had been listening intently although she was known to be unhappy about the new things God was said to be doing by his Spirit. But suddenly, there she was, stretched out on the floor with a positive glow on her face, praising Jesus over and over again.

'Then,' Vanje says happily, 'it was my turn. I can't say I fell down, rather it felt as if my feet came up and I floated. I can't remember any traumatic sensation, just a feeling of being wonderfully cleansed. What I do know and will never, never forget, is that God met me as I lay on the floor of my own home oblivious of the crowds around me, and he totally and completely healed me! He did it all. How I praise him.'

What an evening it was in the Kempster home. When the crowd had dispersed, Vanje, feeling as high as a kite, ordered pizza and ate it and kept it down with no effort. She slept with no gloves on and with no sickness. She got up next morning and with deliberate eagerness and joy cleaned the conservatory and worked with the soil and touched all the plants and nothing happened to her hands.

'God completely healed me as soon as I was prayed for,' she tells, 'And from that time I have had no skin lesions, no stomach pain and never the slightest desire for a drink. And what is more, my relationship with Brian and his with me has been new and wonderful since that day. I can never thank and praise God enough for what he has done for me and for what he is still doing. My only regret is that I lived without him for so long and made such a mess of life. Now my only desire is that I should be used for his glory for the rest of my days.'

I was a sceptic

Oscar Fernandez is a qualified teacher who now works for the Greater London Council. He is of Indian origin but came to England after completing his education in Kenya. He and his wife, Melba, live in South London.

Oscar began to stir as the general anaesthetic wore off. Where was he? What had happened? As his mind cleared he remembered. He had been in the thick of a hockey game, enjoying it to the full when something, the ball or a hockey stick, had smashed into his knee and poleaxed him to the ground. And it was his bad knee, too. As he lay in the hospital bed he counted up the different times that knee had been dislocated in games of football and it came to nine. Nine times he could remember being caught by the searing pain as the bones slipped out of place and tore at the ligaments. And now this.

Turning his head he saw a little bottle beside his bed. What on earth . . .? He called the nurse across and let her know he was conscious and then she saw him looking at the little bottle.

'The doctor thought you'd like that as a souvenir,' she told him and then smiled. 'It's the pieces of smashed and torn off material they found when they opened up your knee.'

Oscar turned his head away. Of all the rotten luck. He couldn't, he wouldn't give up sport. Sport was his life and joy. His family had brought him over to Kenya from Goa in Portuguese India when he was only three or four years old to give him a better chance in life. And he had taken every opportunity offered him. But even in school it was the playing field that had attracted him more than anything else and he had been elected to play for junior teams and senior teams in cricket and all the major sports.

His mind went back to that morning and the joy and excitement that always filled him when a match was coming up. Now it was no longer school games but the real thing. He was a college student and in the college team but also played in club games and, highest of honours, had been elected as the youngest player in Kenya's 1st Division football team.

The game was going well and he was putting everything he had into it when, wham! and it was all over for him. The pain was so severe he hardly remembered being carted off to this very hospital and, with only a cursory look at the injury, he had had his whole leg set in plaster and been sent back to college. But the pain was terrible and with the plaster holding it rigid he didn't know what to do with himself. Eventually, when he couldn't stand it any longer, he'd told Mr Clement, the Principal, all about it and he had brought him straight back to the hospital and demanded a proper examination. And now he was grounded. For how long, he wondered? He didn't have long to wait to be told. With the rather maddening way some doctors have of smiling as they shatter your life, he was told, 'he would probably never take part in active sport again.'

Oscar made up his mind not to accept that verdict and very soon began training and exercising his knee with every intention of getting back on the playing field. But he was not greatly encouraged. He had a shocking limp and couldn't master it and eight years were to pass before he tried again to be actively involved in sport.

Up to that time the family had lived in Nairobi, but eventually Oscar moved to another town called Kitale and soon after he got there he started training with a hockey club. But he had problems. He played a little but his bad knee would suddenly lock and he couldn't go on. Then it began to lock even when he was walking and he knew something was wrong that was going to need further attention. He shared this with an elderly British Army doctor one day and to his great disappointment he was taken into hospital for a further operation and another collection of loose bits and pieces was removed from his knee.

Following another move Oscar again found friends in a hockey club and tried once more to take part in the sport but it was no good. His knee was really bad and he realised he'd had it as far as playing was concerned so gave up hope of serious involvement.

When not on the playing field, Oscar had studied hard and qualified as a teacher. He had also met a lovely girl student called Melba who was to become his wife. They married, gave much thought to their future, and in 1974 moved to London, England, to start a new life together. But their dreams were not fully realised. They were unable to find the teaching jobs for which they were qualified, they were also unable to have the family they so desired. With one thing and another, life was not what they thought it would be. They tried. Both Oscar and Melba had been brought up in the Catholic church, baptised, learned the catechism, and gone to church each week, but that was all. Once their Sunday visit to church was over, the rest of the week was godless. Surely there must be more to religion than that, they thought? But they didn't know what they were looking for and things began to go wrong in their marriage. Little disagreements developed into all out rows. Hurts were nursed and taken personally. They were loyal to each other and didn't look for companionship elsewhere but all the while they were building up barriers of resentment and bitterness and unforgiveness. Somehow there was no knowledge of the power of God that is available to those who really know him. They realised that the same tongues that received the Eucharist were used to lash out at each other and say cruel and unkind things. The same was true of their minds. It seemed such a mockery to go and worship God and then think the nastiest things about each other and other people.

Perhaps it was the desire to get out of this situation that found Oscar once more attempting to take up sport? He had a personal philosophy which was to forget the pain and think of the game. The friends he made thought he was crazy even to try as it was obvious his knee had taken a hammering. One look at it was enough to show that. And they were right.

Just as his game was improving the same old problem cropped up. His knee locked. Once again those chips of cartilage and bone broke away and brought him to a standstill. By this time Oscar had had enough nonsense from his old injuries so he made enquiries as to the very best place to go and found himself at the Royal National Orthopaedic Hospital.

'This knee needs the very best medical skill,' he told the doctor who examined him, and added as a challenge, 'No one has been able to do a good job on it.'

He certainly got the very best medical skill. After examination he was wheeled off once more to the operating theatre where a Harley Street doctor set about remedying the damage. Next day he came to Oscar's bedside.

'What ever did you do to that knee?' he asked. 'Everything was wrong with it. We had to scrape every part in there and screw bits together.' Then he, too, gave Oscar his cheerful verdict. 'The only thing I can promise you is arthritis,' he said.

Once home the knee began to improve and after three months seemed OK but Oscar had utter faith in the doctor's prediction of doom and when, some six months after the operation the pain began again he told Melba the arthritis was starting already.

That was about the time Oscar and Melba heard that new things were happening in some of the churches which friends thought might help them. They certainly needed help from somewhere. After ten years of bickering and fighting and family rifts, the outlook was bleak. If they couldn't find some answers they knew their marriage would join the flood of marriages going down the drain. Oscar summed it up by saying it was possible to live with only one good leg but if you have a rotten mind, that's terrible. So, with many reservations they began to attend Westminster Cathedral.

What they heard and saw amazed them. People actually seemed to enjoy the services. But in spite of the example before them Oscar was very very cautious and certainly not warm to this Renewal or whatever it was he saw before him. At the time he thought it might be alright for other people but not for him! But nevertheless, Sunday by Sunday they got up and ready for church and once again travelled into London to the Cathedral.

One day Oscar felt the limit had been reached. He had hardly taken the new type of worship fully in his stride when he and Melba were invited to a special service at which someone called Ian Andrews was to speak. It was bad enough to hear that this man was an accountant and not even a priest, but when he was told that people would be healed by God in the service Oscar felt his intellectual barriers rising. However, he agreed to go and on the night he and Melba sat looking around to see who else had come along. There were people with braces and calipers and twisted bodies and many who were obviously very sick. Almost as a concession to God Oscar murmured a brief prayer, 'Lord, please heal them,' but he didn't think for a minute that his prayer would be answered. Certainly he never gave a thought to pray for himself, in fact, looking at the needy people around him it never occured to him to bother God with something as trivial as his old knee injury. To be honest, he was very sceptical that anything would happen at all.

After a time of worship and praise Oscar watched as the speaker stepped forward to talk to the large number present. And straight away he felt more at ease. He had been afraid that Ian Andrews would turn out to be a born orator who kept his audience spell-bound and imposed a mass hypnosis on his hearers. But this man had a stammer and what's more he simply talked. Talked of things in the Bible. Talked about Jesus – as if he knew him. It was the very simplicity of the approach that convinced Oscar this was real and melted away his scepticism.

He listened with interest as Ian explained about the Children of Israel in the wilderness and their dilemma when they had no water to drink. In the blistering heat water was vital to keep them alive and there was great joy when they came across the waters at Marah. But their joy was shortlived because the water was bitter and undrinkable. Many tried to drink. After all they had been three whole days with no fresh water. But it was putrid and bitter and a death trap. What could they do? Of course one thing they did was blame Moses who cried to God in prayer for guidance and received an immediate and extraordinary answer to his prayer. God showed him a tree and told him to throw it in the water and, immediately, the water was made pure and fresh.

Ian told how this tree was symbolic of the cross on which Jesus was to die many years later. And he explained how the Lord at Marah had made a covenant with the people. If they would listen to what God had to say and obey what he told them, then the Lord gave his word he would keep them free from disease and sickness. He even gave one of his great names, 'I am the Lord, your healer.'

Everything that was said gave Oscar new thoughts and a fresh understanding of God's will for the saving of souls and the healing of bodies. Ian stressed that God's plan was for the whole person otherwise it was not a big enough plan for Almighty God. Then he brought the climax of that plan before them in a way Oscar had never thought possible.

Ian taught how man is saved from sin by Jesus' death on the cross but had that been the whole of God's plan then the suffering of Jesus at the whipping post would have been unnecessary cruelty. Quoting from Matthew 8 v. 17 Ian drew their attention to the fact that Jesus 'himself took our infirmities and bore our sicknesses.'

Oscar wondered how many times he had read that chapter but had never noticed the quotation Matthew had used from Isaiah 53. But Ian moved on to I Peter 2 v. 24 where, after declaring the act of salvation through the cross, Peter clearly states, 'by whose stripes ye were healed.' Speaking of those stripes or lashes Jesus bore Ian asked his listeners to visualize Jesus strapped to the whipping post and having the nine leather thongs with pieces of bone or glass on the end lashed across his back over and over again.

It was while Ian was bringing this scene to life in all its brutality that a sentence he said went deep into Oscar's thoughts. He said, 'Christ will heal you because he took those lashes for your healing.' As Oscar sat there, his mind caught up in what he was hearing, he suddenly became aware of severe pain in his knee. And at that precise moment Ian broke into what he was saying and pointed in Oscar's direction.

'There's a man over there who has had a terrible knee for years,' he said. But Oscar looked behind to see if anyone was going to acknowledge what Ian had said. No one moved. Then Ian repeated himself and asked the person in question to respond. Still Oscar kept quiet but his thoughts began to race. With three hundred people there, how could Ian pick on him, he didn't even know him. And anyhow, there were people there who were crying to God for healing, surely the Lord wouldn't be so generous as to heal him when he hadn't even asked for healing?

'Will the gentleman with the damaged knee please stand

up?' Ian asked, breaking into Oscar's thoughts. Still he didn't move, making the mental excuse that he wanted to be certain he was the one.

'If the gentleman will please stand up, I'll tell him which knee is the damaged one. In fact it is the right knee and I will be glad if he will stand because then my right knee will stop paining me.'

Reluctantly Oscar rose to his feet.

'I'm the man with the damaged knee,' he said, then added, 'But I'm a bit sceptical about this. I don't know whether I am healed or not.'

Right across the listening crowd Ian declared,

'You are healed. Bang your foot on the floor and you will find there is no pain.'

Oscar banged his foot down hard and certainly there was not the pain he had felt a few moments before. Then he sank back in his seat stunned by what had happened.

Before leaving the Cathedral that night Oscar made his way to Ian and again expressed his doubts as to his healing.

'You are healed,' Ian assured him. 'Really healed. There is not one damaged cartilage or even one cartilage missing, God has given you a good sound knee.'

Oscar went home in a daze. He felt he could believe for freedom from pain after what he had heard in Ian's talk, but that the knee should be as good as new was more than he could take. For days he could think of nothing else and his mind worked on his experience from every angle. He began testing the knee by leaping half a flight of stairs onto his right leg. Even at work he cleared half a flight of metal steps in one great bound. Still no pain. Then he had what he thought was an answer. Of course, cartilage did not show up on an X-ray so there could be no proof the knee was perfect. He admits now that he was a real doubting Thomas but as time has passed he has repented of his scepticism and asked God's forgiveness. The knee has never troubled him again. His testimony today is,

'Our lives have been completely changed. God healed my knee that night, but he has also healed our marriage and our spirits. Our lives, which were becoming unbearable, are now full of the love of Christ. We keep finding more and more good things in life to enjoy. We are not angels! But out of the goodness of the Lord to us spiritually, mentally and physically, we can see the road ahead and it is light.'

God is my rock

Mrs Una Macey has lived in South East England all her life. For a large part of that time she has been involved in nursing of one kind or another while bringing up a family. Now, with her husband retired, she is involved in Christian outreach and the Lydia Prayer Fellowship.

Una Macey pushed her front door shut with a sigh of relief. A blizzard was blowing up outside and it was bitterly cold. But that would not normally have worried her. What was a little disturbing was what had happened during the afternoon. After a lot of preparation a friend had called on that December day in 1978 to give Una final instructions on the best way to run the church library. She was shown what to do and was eager to get started. But she felt so terribly ill. It was all she could do to respond as the job was explained to her but when the friend left a wave of nausea swept over her and she felt really ill. Her ears were buzzing, too, which told Una her blood pressure was high and at one point she thought she was going to faint.

Una's one desire was to get to bed but she felt so weak and desperately tired. The stairs could have been a rocky mountain they looked so ominous, but somehow she climbed them and fell on her bed too exhausted even to pull the covers over her knees. Surely her husband would have left work by now and would be in soon? He would help her. Perhaps he could give her something to take away the tightness and pain in her chest? But the blizzard increased and it was late when he came in and by then she didn't feel quite so bad.

As a nurse herself Una rather brushed aside this unpleasant little episode, even when the doctor told her it seemed she had had a slight coronary thrombosis. She had always been busy and as things cleared up she became busy again. She just wasn't used to sitting around.

Brought up in the country in a happy home, Una expected to be able to live an active life with no restrictions. She had decided nursing was to be her life when encouraged to do a job of value to others during preparation for Confirmation. And at the time when the Bishop laid his hands on her at that service a peace had come into her heart that had convinced her of the love of God the Father though she had no personal knowledge of Jesus Christ at that time.

As soon as she was seventeen Una started nursing in a private nursing home and life was very pleasant. Always a lover of nature, she got out and about in the countryside and when off duty in the evening she liked to go dancing. But her church connection was precious to her, too, and she kept up her attendance whenever possible. At eighteen she began her nursing training and was satisfied and fulfilled in her work until, only a few months before her finals, she fell in love. It was war time. Her soldier boy was going abroad for D-day. What should she do? In the end she gave up her training and married the man she loved. But it wasn't the end of her nursing career as Una joined the Civil Nursing Reserve to wait for her husband's return from the war.

Happily he came back unscathed and married life began in the shortages that followed the end of open hostilities. Like so many in the ensuing years, to better themselves meant jolly hard work and eventually her husband took on the mammoth task of building their own bungalow while continuing to hold a responsible job. But a project like that costs a lot of money so Una, now the mother of two fine sons, went back to nursing two nights a week to help with the finances.

Perhaps the weariness that had dogged her over recent years really went back to those two nights on duty and the busyness and responsibilities of her family in the daytime. Certainly she grew tired and irritable all those years earlier and felt as if she might crack up. But God has his ways of fulfilling his plan for our lives. The two boys wanted to go to the Cubs but the only Cub pack was at a different church to the one Una attended. 'Please can we go, Mummy?' the boys begged and added that the minister joked with them and was full of life and even knew them by name! So along they went both to the Cubs and Sunday School and loved it. But before long they came back talking about a Family Service and 'you will come, won't you?' Una went and, following a visit from the boys' Sunday School Teacher, she also went to the Young Wives Fellowship and enjoyed that. At first she made the excuse that her life was work, work, work and church would make a change. But before long she went because she wanted to go and it was not long before she committed her life to Jesus Christ. After that Una became involved in the church in a big way.

Which was why she was taking over the library that cold cold day when she felt so ill. It was also why she didn't let up but was persuaded to take over a group of lively teenagers in the Sunday School not long after her coronary warning. Perhaps to appease her conscience Una resigned from a one day a week nursing job at a nearby school, but the rest gained from letting that go was more than offset by her involvement with the teenagers.

It wasn't only at the church that Una became involved either. Like many other women, she felt called to pray for our nation with the Lydia Prayer Fellowship and also travelled up to London to the Caring Professions Seminars for Christians in the medical world. As Jesus himself said, 'the harvest is ready but the workers are few.' But some workers carry loads heavier than our human frame can bear. Even after Una had the empowering experience of the filling with the Holy Spirit back in 1977 at a Lydia Conference there were physical limits beyond which her body began to complain.

Shortly after the sharp warning she received, there was to be a healing service at which the Bishop of Selby was to minister. Una didn't think of what she considered her own slight problem. Instead she suggested to a dear friend that they might go to the service together as her friend was depressed after losing her husband. But before leaving home her husband asked her if she had considered prayer for her own healing. She hadn't, but as the service progressed it seemed to be the right thing to do and on going forward the Bishop laid hands on her and her chest pain ceased. However, healing from the Lord is not a freedom to break the rules of sensible living as Jesus himself pointed out. The vast crowd he healed on the banks of Galilee were later miraculously fed by him 'so that they did not faint on the way home.' With Una it was her constant activity even beyond her physical strength that caused problems later.

All went well for a couple of years but then, shortly after her husband's retirement, Una picked up a virus that was going around. It was a nasty brute that gave chest pains, thick catarrh and a continual hacking cough. Eventually, when it wouldn't go away, she went to the doctor who assured her it was typical of the bug that was doing the rounds and, to reassure her, checked her blood pressure. That, he told her, was quite normal for her age and told her not to worry about herself as all would be well. But there was a special function coming up to which her husband very much wanted to go. His old firm was holding a dinner dance and all his old friends were to be present. In fact after several months retirement, it was to be a real reunion of old friends and work companions. What's more overnight accommodation was to be provided and it was to be quite a highlight in the rather gloomy month of February. The only question mark over the evening was Una's health and her husband asked her more than once if she was sure she was well enough to go.

Obviously that dinner meant a great deal to her husband and it was clear he would not go and leave her at home alone. And anyway she was a lot better and could see no reason for spoiling the evening, so Una assured him she was well enough and also that she was happy to go on the next day to care for her ninety year old mother-in-law for the weekend as had been planned.

It was an effort to get ready but Una managed it and they went off and had a very enjoyable meal. But the room was hot and stuffy and not long after the dinner ended, Una and another lady who had also been unwell, left the room to sit together in a lounge where the air was fresh and the atmosphere more peaceful. Every so often her husband came to see if she was all right and to ask her if she wished to go up and get to bed. But Una convinced herself that she was resting as she sat there quietly and was unwilling to cut short her husband's pleasure. But as time went on that deathly weariness came over her and the chest pains she had thought were the virus increased and caused her considerable discomfort. Like so many others, Una thought that if she ignored them they would go away.

It was the early hours when the party eventually broke up and after a cup of coffee, everyone made their way up to bed. Una and her husband went to their room tired from the long day and ready for a good sleep after all the talk and excitement. Within a few minutes her husband had washed and rolled into bed on the side near the telephone and dropped into a deep, satisfied sleep. Una was washing herself and doing all the things women do when suddenly she had the most crushing, terrible chest pain. Doubled up in agony and unable to scarcely move, let alone call out, she knew that this time she had the real thing, a serious coronary attack. There was a young man among the guests who had had a coronary and she desperately wished she could somehow get to him and take one of the pills she knew he carried to relieve the pain. She couldn't call out, she couldn't reach the phone to ring for a doctor or an ambulance. So she did the only thing she could do in the circumstances, she prayed. 'Lord, help me,' she cried from the depths of her being and at that the pain eased a little. Crawling into bed she lay still, seeking to relax, talking to the Lord, longing for morning.

But when morning came and the crisis had apparently passed, she agreed to continue to her mother-in-law's home where her husband did the work and Una did as little as possible on account of the pain in her chest.

It was with considerable relief that they eventually reached home again where Una rested and took things quietly promising herself she would go back to the doctor if the pain did not go. In the day she rested and found strength and comfort by reading her Bible, but by evening she was too exhausted even for that so asked the Lord to give her a verse to help her. Into her mind immediately came the lovely promise, 'I have loved you with an everlasting love.' So she clung to this verse night and morning and began to do little jobs around the house.

Then, one day, nearly three weeks later, Una again felt very very ill and actually collapsed. Her husband called the doctor urgently and first one came and then another and before very long an ambulance was taking Una off to the hospital at high speed. There tests were carried out and she was told she was to be admitted to the Intensive Care Coronary Unit. But word gets round of these crises and while the tests were in progress the family gathered and with them the minister and his assistant from Una's church. By now they all knew Una's condition was serious but it was a time for prayer and not for panic and Peter, the minister, took Una by the hand while the nurse stood waiting and earnestly prayed for healing in spirit, mind and body. That was all. But it was a prayer that was heard and answered because, not only did Una experience an amazing peace and freedom from fear, but she was convinced of the presence of the angels of God as she was wheeled away and strung up to all the monitors and infusions medically necessary. And prayer continued both at the church and round the country through the Lydia Prayer Fellowship.

Meanwhile, away in the seclusion of the Intensive Care Unit, Una was resting in the Lord and depending on him. Managing to read her Bible the next day she came on a wonderful promise which she believed to be a direct message from God to her. The very next morning a letter came from a friend quoting the same verse and confirming to Una that it was God's love-letter to her. It comes from Daniel 10. vv 17-19 and reads, ''How can I, your servant, talk with you, my Lord? My strength is gone and I can hardly breathe.' Again the one who looked like a man touched me and gave me strength. 'Do not be afraid, O man highly esteemed,' he said. 'Peace! Be strong now; be strong.' When he spoke to me, I was strengthened and said, 'Speak, my lord, since you have given me strength.'' God could not have found a more appropriate promise and Una's spirit was able to rest on these words.

Further tests and a lung scan were carried out and then one day the doctor in charge of the team carrying out treatment came in, flanked by two of his colleagues. He looked at Una seriously and told her, 'The results of the tests are not very encouraging. You have several blood clots in your lungs. You will be given intensive treatment.' Una asked him if he thought the treatment would be successful but he would not commit himself. Suddenly Una felt as if she were plunged into darkness. Up to that point she had only sought answers from the Lord. Now she had turned to a man who felt unable to give an answer. As a nurse she knew she was seriously ill and might die at any moment. For a few moments she battled in her spirit as she thought of her husband and sons, her daughters-in-law and lovely grandchildren. She thought of the joy of going to her Lord, then of her sisters and friends. But as she felt herself slipping into fear the Word of God came to her, 'As thy days so shall thy strength be' – 'My grace is sufficient for thee' – 'My strength is made perfect in weakness' – 'you are on a Rock which cannot be moved, I am that Rock, Christ Jesus.' Promise after promise flowed into her spirit and lifted her into praise and peace and joy. Although critically ill and attached to a machine for treatment Una was so overwhelmed by the reality of her relationship with God that she was able to rest in her faith without a trace of fear from that time on.

Two weeks after admission Una was discharged, weak, still with some pain and with plenty of pills to take with her. She was worried that she would probably have to take pills for the rest of her life. She had to return to the haematology department at the hospital frequently and rest most of the time at home but little by little she began to move around and it was not long before she ventured to the bottom of the garden. But a bit too much exertion set her back and also kept her dependent on her Bible for encouragement. On one occasion when the pain in her chest was particularly severe Una was led to read Psalm 91 and was tremendously strengthened by the promise of the Lord's care, that he was her Shield and Buckler. So, by faith she took the Shield to cover her heart and the Buckler to reach up and protect her other trouble area, her lungs. From that time the improvement was slow but steady toward normal life and a reduction of medication.

After all Una had passed through it was natural to her to join in praying for a visit of Ian Andrews who was coming to the local Baptist Church for a healing service in June 1980. She was able to attend prayer sessions two or three times and also encouraged others to attend the meeting. On the evening of the meeting she took a friend who had severe back trouble and they joined the many people who filled the church. A crowd always gives a special atmosphere, but a crowd singing the praises of God is very special and prepares the way for the message of God to be shared. That evening Ian gave a basic talk about healing starting with the Children of Israel coming out of Egypt to begin their journey through the desert to the Promised Land. He told how they had become desperate for water and eventually came to an oasis only to find the water there undrinkable. How Moses had cried to God for help and was instructed to throw a nearby length of tree into the water and when he obeyed it became pure. Then how God had made a covenant with the people that if they would obey him completely, he would be their healer and keep them free from the diseases around them. 'The problem is,' Ian said, 'that Jesus must be made Lord in order that a Christian may receive his blessings.' Ian warned that a lot of people have the idea that Jesus can be their Saviour and they only need to make him Lord when they are old and have had their own way for much of their life.

Going on with the journey of the Children of Israel through the desert, Ian told how the people began to complain and speak against Moses and against God until God became angry with them. He sent fiery, red snakes among the people and many of them died, but in his mercy God told Moses to make a bronze serpent and put it on a pole. Any who looked away from their sickness and gazed at the pole would be healed. What a test that was. If they didn't obey they died, but in order to be healed they had to believe what God was saying and act on it.

In the same way Jesus was going to be lifted up on a cross and Ian explained that people today must be like the Children of Israel who received their healing. They have to look at all that Jesus accomplished at the cross with their whole concentration. They have to forget their sickness and think only of him because at the Cross he dealt with every sickness and disease as well as every sin.

Sitting in the church listening, Una became caught up with the picture Ian painted of Jesus' sufferings.

As the teaching drew to a close, Jesus was very present by his Holy Spirit and began to give words of knowledge to Ian which he declared to all present. Suddenly he said, 'Someone here has been healed of a blood condition.' Una took notice and began to think. She hadn't felt anything and she knew there was another person there with an anaemic condition, but it might mean God had completed her own healing. Perhaps, after all, even the pills might become a thing of the past.

Making her way home that night Una had a lovely peace and decided that she would soon know if God had finally restored her to wholeness. She certainly felt well and knew without a doubt that God was able to heal her, but it would be proved when she had her next blood test at the clinic. But nothing was said, until three weeks later, when the doctor told her that she might well be off all medication after her next visit to the specialist. Then he added, 'I noticed that your tests on your last visit were very satisfactory.'

With joy Una went to the specialist and found him all smiles. Sure enough he told her, 'You'll be pleased to know you are coming off the last tablets. In fact you don't need to come anymore. You are discharged fit.'

In six months Una had travelled from death's door via much love and prayer and resting on the promises of God, to full health. In fact, as she says, 'It's the Almighty, the Lord Jesus.' And so it is, because today Una walks in perfect health and full of the praises of Jesus.

Our God is great

Walther Jessen is an ordained priest of the church in Denmark. He served as a missionary in Nigeria for many years before having to return home through ill health.

'At first I thought I was only tired. It was hot out in Nigeria where my wife and I were living, but that was nothing new. We had been working as missionaries with the Sudan Mission for fifteen years and were used to the heat and the conditions of this tropical African country. Nor could it be that I was particularly over weary. In the years we had lived and worked in Nigeria we had learned our limitations and saw to it that we didn't overstep the limits of our strength. But the symptoms persisted and eventually I went to the doctors only to find they were as puzzled as I was myself. The various tests and examinations I was subjected to threw no light on the cause of my problem so eventually and sadly we were obliged to return to our home country of Denmark.

'Once home I trained and became an ordained priest in Denmark, but in 1963 the tropical disease that had been troubling me consistently broke out in my skin and my wife and I realised that it could well be a case of leprosy. About that time our very good friend in Nigeria came home and, as he had been the medical missionary in our area, we consulted him. Of course a lot of tests were made and samples sent to the Institute of Tropical Diseases in London, England. We were left in no doubt after that, the diagnosis was clear. I had leprosy.

'Somehow there is a particular stigma attached to this disease in the European countries whereas in Africa there are many thousands of cases treated by government and mission hospitals and clinics. There was a time when little was known of the disease and consequently little could be done by way of treatment. But today all that has changed. There are clinics and control units working in all the countries where the disease is prevalent and medical research has discovered the treatment that will keep the disease in check.

'But I was no longer in Africa, I was in Denmark and as far as I knew, I was the only case of leprosy recorded in my home country. What is more I was priest in my church and constantly in contact with my parishioners. However, as soon as a firm diagnosis had been made I had no choice and retired from my duties for eighteen months while the correct medication for my condition was prescribed and applied. Once under control and the disease arrested I was no longer infectious or contagious and I was able to return to my duties in my church and parish.

'Many years passed and I faithfully took my pills and carried out my priestly duties. But in all this time of more than twelve years, I never told anyone what was really wrong with me. If someone asked after my health I passed off my problems as a tropical disease that I had picked up. After all, these people trusted me and I was the one who christened their babies and celebrated communion with them. My secret was a burden to me but my experience in Africa assured me that there was no way I could pass on the leprosy to others when it was arrested in my own case.

However, in 1978 I began having severe pains in my stomach and then again the skin lesions of leprosy broke out. Over the years it was clear that I had become immune to the medicine I had been given. Once again samples were taken and sent over to London and I was told I must go back into hospital, to be reassessed and a different treatment prescribed.

'That was when God stepped in because at that precise time I had arranged some meetings in my church, Fredens Kirke, when Ian Andrews was coming from England to speak on the subject, 'Jesus Heals Today.' The meeting was planned weeks earlier but it turned out that my hospital admittance was to be the day following Ian's visit. The church filled up and there was an air of expectancy as he went through a time of worship and praise before Ian stood up to speak.

' 'Jesus Christ is the same yesterday, and today and for ever.' he began, quoting from Hebrews 13 v. 8. 'Because Jesus Christ is for ever the same, he heals people today basically in the same three ways he healed people when he lived on this earth in human form.

' 'Sometimes a person is simply touched by the Lord. As Jesus passes by, he looks into the person's heart and says, 'I think I'll heal you. I think you have been sick long enough. I think I'll just reach down and touch you.' And immediately there is health and restoration.

' 'Other people have to reach out and touch the Lord. And to do this they have to get beyond barriers of fear and discouragement. They have to face up to resentment and bitterness over their problem and surmount the very big obstacle of self-pity. It is as if God loves them too much to heal them until they have dealt with these hindrances and are ready to press in to God and touch the very hem of Jesus' garment. Then something inexplicable medically takes place.

' 'But most of the time Jesus didn't pray for people, he went around speaking the words of God and the word he spoke was Spirit and life and carried the gift of healing to the sick person. When Jesus was speaking of the end times, he said, 'Heaven and earth shall pass away, but my words shall not pass away.' Matthew 24 v. 35. The word Jesus speaks today has lost none of its power. But God is very gentle, 100% supernatural and about nil % spectacular. When he heals it is over so quickly you haven't time to see the miracle. One minute you are sick, the next you are well. It's marvellous!' he continued as everyone listened.

'At the close of that meeting many were healed and I sat watching and praying earnestly that Jesus would heal me, too. But the meeting ended and there had been no word of knowledge from God relating to my secret problem. But somehow I felt it was a vital night for me and I might never have another opportunity like it. My admittance to the hospital the next day was in the back of my mind all evening. As I sat there it seemed that God was waiting for me to take the initiative.

'The crowd dispersed slowly and then Ian Andrews, Svend Boysen, the Pastor of the Danish Evangelical-Lutheran Church at Give, and I went through into the vestry. There I told them of my leprosy and asked for prayer. Together they laid hands on me and prayed that I would be healed 'in Jesus' Name.' We went home and, with my heart full of wonder and praise, I realised that the severe pains in my stomach had already gone.

'The next day I was admitted to hospital and all the tests were begun again. But our faithful and loving God had intervened. The tests were negative and after less than three weeks I was discharged and told I could go back to my work! How we praised the Lord. There was only one difficulty. For fear of misunderstanding I still held back from sharing what the Lord had done for me with my parishioners.

'It was a year later, a year of praise and physical wholeness, that once again Ian Andrews and Svend Boysen paid a return visit to our church. The service took a different form to their first visit because Ian asked those who had been healed the previous year to stand up and give testimony of their healing. One by one those who had been healed rose to their feet and gave the glory of God. And after each one I said, 'Hallelujah! Our God is great! And the heavens answer,' . . . 'Amen!' responded the entire congregation. Meanwhile, in all this joy and praise, God was challenging me in my heart to declare before all present what he had done for me. It was a testing point for me and a difficult thing to do. Eventually I was willing and rose to my feet.

' 'I have to make a confession to you all,' I began. 'I have lied to you regarding my illness over the years. I was afraid to tell you what was wrong with me in case you felt you could not come to me. But now I tell you. I had leprosy, but Jesus has healed me. Hallelujah! How great is our God. And the heavens answer,' . . .

' 'AMEN!' came like a trumpet of praise from all present.

'Since then I have been privileged to experience time after time God's intervention in people's lives and the evidence of his healing power.

'He is still the Saviour of the whole person, spirit, soul and body. And our praise song must indeed be, 'Hallelujah! How great is our God. And the heavens reply, 'Amen!' '

Double blessing

Glenn and Chrissie Longhurst live in the Midlands of England. Glenn is co-leader of a house church that meets in a church building. They have three children, two of them adopted and the story is of God's touch on both the adopted children.

It was a sad day when Chrissie Longhurst's baby was stillborn. As young parents, she and Glenn had eagerly awaited their first child. All the clothes and baby things were ready, but their joy ended when it should have just begun. And things got worse. The doctors gently told them that Chrissie's condition was such that she should have no more babies. Glenn worked in an office at the time and it grieved him to leave his young wife each morning knowing there was no little one to bring her joy and for them to watch grow and develop and take a place in this world.

They were Christians when they married and this was a real testing time for their faith, which was not too strong at the time anyway. They described themselves as 'Sunday Christians' meaning they were happy to attend church regularly but it didn't make a great deal of difference to the rest of the week.

As the pain of their loss began to ease, their thoughts turned to the many children without a family and a couple of years after losing their baby, they became registered foster parents and took a baby into their home for short-term fostering. Then a second baby was put in their care, a tiny, red-headed baby girl. A baby girl with a difference. Little Julie was a Down's syndrome baby, or as the layman calls it, she was a mongoloid baby. Glenn and Chrissie hadn't entertained the idea of fostering a baby with a problem, but here was Julie, in their home and as soon as they saw her they fell in love with her and a deep desire to keep her grew in their hearts. They talked about the idea, they constantly thought about the future for themselves and Julie, and they prayed very much for guidance as to what they should do. Julie's own parents were very young but they were open about the fact that they did not feel able to cope with Julie's problem. But what future was there for that six week old baby if her parents felt unable to care for her and Glenn and Chrissie shut the door on her? It was impossible to quench the love in their hearts and turn her away. They decided to aim towards adopting her and eleven years later freely admit that the Lord has really blessed that decision.

As with many Down's syndrome babies, Julie was quite difficult to rear. It took a long time to feed her and often the feed came back as soon as it was completed. When she got beyond the bottle she would often end up screaming at meal times if someone touched her food. There was no weakness in her will! But she was loved, deeply loved, so much so that Glenn and Chrissie applied for a second baby when Julie was two years old and then aimed at adoption of both Julie and Paul who joined the family when he was six weeks old. Paul also was a red-head and Paul also had problems, but Glenn and Chrissie knew they were doing right and being fulfilled in making a home in the real sense for these gifts from God.

About the time Paul joined the family, Julie began to walk and when she was three she went along daily to a special school for mentally handicapped children where there were others for her to play with. Like many mongoloid children she was very loving but there was another side to her that caused considerable concern both at home and at school. When upset little Julie would set on the other children and sometimes gripped them by the throat, refusing to let go. It was impossible to reason with her so that sent Glenn and Chrissie to the Lord in prayer for help. Julie had enough difficulties in life without being violent and the school were anxious as to how she would develop. But our great God had no problem over the situation and he answered Glenn and Chrissie's call for help by taking away the aggression which has never returned. He answered another heartfelt prayer, too.

While petite little Julie was slowly progressing, Paul was very disturbed and suffered frequent and horrific nightmares. He would cry a great deal and, as he grew a little older, would refuse to go to bed, scared in case he had a bad dream. Glenn and Chrissie knew these were the results of his difficult start in life, but by now they also knew where to turn for an answer. One night when Paul was sleeping soundly they went together into his room and commanded the devil to leave their child in the name of Jesus, telling the enemy to take all his evil influences with him. A few years earlier they would not have thought of taking such action, or if they had thought of it they would not have dared to do such a thing. But in 1974 when Julie was four and Paul two years old, both these young parents had experienced the blessing of God by the filling with his Spirit. So that night they prayed with faith and they prayed with authority and as they completed their task, little Paul's face softened and his problems lessened at once. Only on one occasion after that did he have another nightmare and they treated it for what it was, a deliberate attack to test their faith. It was also in 1974 that Paul became a full member of the family, his adoption having gone through the official channels very quickly. Not so with Julie. With her they met with rather more complications but they were cleared up by the time she was five and the family seemed to be complete.

However, our God of love had a special treat in store. As Glenn and Chrissie moved ahead in the things of the Spirit of God, they also prayed and believed for God's healing touch for Chrissie and, in 1975, the year Julie became their own, they were also blessed with a son, Jamin. It was as if God made their cup of joy run over by rounding off the family with their own son eight years after losing their first baby.

Now everything appeared set for normal family life. Very slowly Julie was making progress though she remained so small that this caused some concern. Paul was growing well in body and every way and the hurts of the past were healing. Jamin was all they could wish for, strong and healthy and a joy to them all. But Glenn and Chrissie are not normal people and once again they opened their house to take in someone in need. With their living faith, they were unable to shut the door on those less fortunate than they were. And this was God's preparation for the revealing of his plan for their lives. There came a day after much prayer, study and consultation, when Glenn came home from the office for the last time and he and Chrissie left the ranks of the secular workers to become full-time co-workers with God in reaching out to others. They had seen such wonderful answers to prayer in their own home that this was clearly to be their next step. Constant prayer for Julie was steadily expanding her. Paul had come to a personal faith in Jesus. Their home was used in whatever way the Lord led. Now was the time to step out and trust him for everything.

Then, when Paul was six, he had a friend come and stay with him for a week and they had a wonderful time playing together and enjoying each other's company. No one thought that a long-term problem lay ahead for Paul. But quite soon after this, Glenn and Chrissie noticed Paul was limping and the limp persisted until one day he came in from school in tears and complaining of pain in his hip. It took two months to diagnose the cause of the pain which turned out to be a rare condition called Perthe's Disease when the bone in the hip joint softens. The treatment is rest and occasionally an operation but if the condition is ignored there is the likelihood of arthritis in later years. So energetic six year old Paul had to become a semi invalid with a sling from his shoulders down to support his foot and keep his leg bent up behind so no weight went on it. Of course this made it necessary for him to use crutches. This went on for more than a year. Back and forth, to and from the hospital went Chrissie with their two chosen children. Julie went for a check up every six months and Paul was under constant observation. But with all this going on, the parent's faith and expectancy that God would touch these children in his own good time never waivered.

It was autumn 1980 when an opportunity to reach out in faith in a new way came along. Two meetings had been arranged in their fellowship and Ian Andrews had been invited to speak. Because of the family Chrissie was not able to go on the Saturday night but Glenn told her what had been said when he came in that evening. After giving his testimony, Ian had talked at length about the sufferings of Jesus at the time of the crucifixion and had told how he saw more and more of all that Jesus had borne on our behalf. Starting in the garden of Gethsemane, Jesus had gone through such agony of mind at the knowledge that he was to be made sin for us that he even sweat drops of blood. Meditating on this, God had revealed to Ian that this was to redeem us from the curse put on Adam in the garden of Eden after he had sinned. God told Adam that he would live by the sweat of his brow from then on and since that time man has lived under tension, anxiety and mental stress, even retardation. When Jesus sweat blood it was to redeem us from these states of mind.

There was much for Glenn and Chrissie to think and pray about. Up to that time they had known that God could and would heal physical sickness and disease, but had been unsure about mental healing. If they could both believe for Julie and 'see' her in their spirits whole and well, then they felt it would be right for them to ask for prayer and believe for God's touch.

By morning they were agreed about this and set off as a family, Paul still with a marked limp, to go to hear Ian speak. It was to be a Sunday to remember. There were quite a lot of children present and Ian talked about the blessing given to a child when the Holy Spirit is a living reality right through the school years. He spoke of the stresses that face the children of today and the academic standards they are encouraged to reach. If only they are sensitive to the Holy Spirit in their lives and able to communicate with God in the power of the Holy Spirit, what a difference this makes. 'God is intensely practical,' Ian told them. 'Take him into your everyday life by faith and he will bless you.' He went on to encourage his listeners by assuring them that while gross darkness covers the earth these days, the light of God is on his people and they are ascending to their places of authority and power. But, Ian stressed, the key to this authority and power is God's love. God's love in his people poured in by the Holy Spirit within. And he reminded his listeners that fear and love cannot live together so to lead a child to the filling by God's Spirit of love will keep them from the fear that is all around.

As the service progressed Ian began to call out those with sicknesses that God was revealing to him. But as it was a meeting specially directed toward the children, he asked the children to pray for some of the sick ones and God healed them. This was not an act of showmanship, but a demonstration that it is the Holy Spirit who is doing the healing and not any one person.

Glenn and Chrissie were watching all that was taking place, waiting for God's guidance for their family needs. Then, to their joy, Paul limped up to Ian who asked him if he would like to be healed. Would he? Measuring Paul's legs as he sat on a chair revealed a distinct lopsidedness but, before Ian had finished praying the legs were restored to the same length and God had completed the healing in the hip.

'Clear a passage,' Ian told the children and then, turning to Paul, 'Off you go. Let's see how you walk now that Jesus has healed you.' There was no limp, no roll, no problem, nor has there been from that time.

Before going out that morning Glenn and Chrissie had talked to Julie, asking her if she would like 'Uncle Ian' to pray with her and ask Jesus to make her better. Now seemed the time to go forward. No one knew what to expect. It was a simple, gentle prayer with, of course, no evidence such as growing legs and absence of a limp. But Julie knew what was happening and Glenn and Chrissie had utter faith that God would act. God honoured that faith. Not by some dramatic total restoration, but by very definite signs of the work done deep within. From that time Julie has eaten with a knife and fork with no problem. Before that day she would not attempt to use anything but a spoon. Now Julie thinks things out. Going to the car shortly after being prayed for, Julie found the door locked. But, instead of standing waiting as she would previously have done, she opened the front door, reached in, released the lock catch and opened the door herself. She is reading now and tries again when things go wrong instead of giving up in frustration. Before she could not coordinate properly but now her joy in life is to be out playing with a ball among the other children.

But perhaps most noticeable of all to Chrissie at the time was the change in muscle tone. To play next door Chrissie would lift Julie over a small fence and it was quite a task as Julie was a dead weight. After the touch of God's Spirit Chrissie went to lift her over and she was light! Normal, responsive body weight with correct muscle tone.

A year later the evidence was piling up to the glory of God. Julie sings and dances and enjoys being prayed for. She grew three inches in a year and needed new clothes as never before. She reasons things out and is steadily improving on all levels. But it is an ongoing healing and there are improvements still being made. Questions and answers demand her concentration and conversation becomes easier as time passes. But God is in control and he is working in this young life and making something of it that was not thought possible in her early years. And Glenn and Chrissie? They are praising God and still keeping their home open to those in need.

I felt God's touch

Mrs Pauline Stead was born in South Africa. She and her husband, Ian, spent over two years as part of the team in the printing press of a Christian mission in England before returning to South Africa to work in a pastoral capacity in their home town of Durban.

Pauline lay motionless in a darkened room. The pain in her head was particularly severe and, when she could think at all, it was only to decide whether she could lie still a little longer or whether she should struggle up off the bed to vomit yet again. It was the second time that week that she had woken with a throbbing, burning, frightening headache. But it had happened so many times before. In fact it had been a sinister kind of engagement present to Ian, now her husband. At twenty one years old, while working in a Durban bank, she had met and fallen in love with a young man who was a Bible College student and attended the same church.

They promised to marry and were preparing for the big day while keeping on with their active lives and it was then that Pauline noticed her occasional headaches were recurring with disturbing frequency. She'd had 'a nasty head', as she described it, at intervals through her final year at school but had put it down to normal pressure from exams and study. But it had been an unexpected problem because, although happily average academically, Pauline Cox had excelled on the sports track and been elected Athletic Captain of School. The long jump and high jump had been her star achievements and she gained tremendous satisfaction each time the high jump pole was raised and she beat her rivals by clearing it. It almost became an obsession not only to break her own record but to set a standard of performance that would keep her as number one. But, unknowingly, what was such a joy then paved the way to problems in later years.

As the migraines increased, so the trek to the doctor became more frequent, but, apart from advising aspirin, no X-rays were taken and very little help resulted. A visit to a chiropractor revealed a few misplaced vertebrae but at that time no one suspected a more severe condition. And now there seemed no end to the pain.

Hearing a slight sound as the door opened, Pauline slowly turned her aching head to see Mark, one of her seven year old twin boys standing looking at her, a cup of tea in his hand. Suddenly she wanted to cry. That little boy could see his mother was unwell and had done the only thing he thought might help. On his own he had made a cup of tea and brought it to her.

'Put it on the table, darling,' she murmured. 'Mummy will drink it in a minute.'

'I thought it would make you better.'

'I'm quite sure it will help,' his mother assured him.

But, when the pain eventually eased and she could think again, Pauline wondered what the end of it all would be. Here they were in England, thousands of miles from home, happy as a family and busy at the Mission press, but unable to break free from the recurring and increasingly severe pain. Lying there on the bed Pauline thought again of her younger days. Of one thing she was certain and that was that she would have cracked up completely had it not been for her faith. She could hear again the way she had rebuffed her friends when they visited her to join them at a Christian camp.

'Thanks very much, but I'm not interested in your Youth Camp,' Pauline had said for the umpteenth time.

'But it's terrific,' her friends pressed here. 'We have a great time.'

'Oh, I'm sure you do,' Pauline retaliated. 'With religion morning, noon and night, it must be a real thrill. Let me tell you, I have all the religion I need and believe I am well and truly saved, or whatever you call it.'

'But you're one of us and we want you to come,' her friends persisted. And eventually they won their point and Pauline went to camp. But it was with very mixed feelings as it seemed such a waste of time. It was July, a lovely month in Durban, and Pauline was in her last year at High School. Everything was going her way, surely there was nothing more that life could offer?

To Pauline's surprise she found the camp a time of fun, fulfilment and above all, challenge as the love of Jesus reached her in a way she had never before experienced. And, by the time the end of camp came, Pauline Cox had realised that religion was never going to get her to heaven, that she needed to invite Jesus Christ into her life and make him her Saviour and Lord.

Thinking about it as she lay on her bed with young Mark's love gift of a cup of tea beside her, Pauline turned yet again to the Lord Jesus to ask him what was to be the way out from all this pain that radiated from her head down to her pelvis and right down her legs to her feet. There had to be an answer, but where was it, what was it, how was she to cope with her four children as the pain came with increasing frequency?

Since coming to England Pauline had visited another chiropractor and he had X-rayed her thoroughly and told her the X-ray showed her pelvis to be tipped to one side. He had been the one to find the cause of all the pain at last, but he had been unable to do anything about it. Nor was he able to suggest how the condition had been caused but the more Pauline thought about it, the more she became sure that her whole-hearted involvement in sport, and particularly, jumping, lay at the root of the problem. This was not through the fact of jumping but because the technique of the Western Roll evidently touched on a weak spot and caused damage. Thinking back, Pauline realised that the constant thrust, always on the same side, and the thud of a body-landing must have fractionally misplaced the bones in her back and pelvis. And no doubt the thud of landing in the long jump had added to the injury.

Of course, childbirth hadn't helped, though the babies had not noticeably worsened her condition. She had not known about the misplacement of her pelvis when the first son was born, nor the twins, though about fifteen pounds of baby had to be a strain on any back. But the arrival of a lovely daughter was full of drama. When seven months pregnant, of all things, Pauline caught whooping cough and apparently the baby was compressed against a major blood vessel. By the time for delivery Pauline was utterly exhausted and the severe haemorrhage that occurred when the baby released the pressure on the blood vessel left Pauline in a serious condition for a while. But she pulled through and everything would have been fine but for the severe pain from head to toe.

With four children it was not possible to lie around all day so she coped as best she could, but she would have given a great deal to be free from pain.

Drinking the tea that had gone cold as she lay there, Pauline tried to think what else she could do to get fit and well again.

'I've prayed, my! how I've prayed,' she told herself as she dressed slowly. 'I've been to doctors till I'm ashamed to go again. I've tried spinal manipulation and not found a cure. I've even given up coffee in case that was making me tense and strung up.' She smiled wanly as she pulled on a heavy sweater. A little South African warmth instead of dear old cold England wouldn't be a bad thing, she thought. Always one to tense easily, the chill of a cold morning aggravated her condition until she almost reached screaming point or despair depending on what was going on at the time. Surely, if only for her family's sake, there had to be relief somewhere. Meanwhile she must just grit her teeth and try to live as normal a life as possible.

Another two years passed after the episode with a cup of tea which had touched her so deeply. Then one of her friends at the Mission asked her to come along to a special meeting at a Fellowship they attended. Ian Andrews was coming for a healing meeting. Of course, it would be one of Pauline's bad days when to sit on a hard chair was like sitting on upturned tin tacks!

'I had had a busy day,' she remembers. 'And it was cold and wet and my back was tightening up. As I sat there I was trying to concentrate on what Ian Andrews was saying. His talk was based on the Lord's prayer and he took it bit by bit and made it come alive to the crowd who had gathered to hear him.' But there were sentences that held a special message for Pauline that night. Having spent some time explaining the relationship of Christian with Christian because the prayer begins with that inclusive word, 'Our', Ian moved on to bring out the wonder of our God being our perfect, wonderful, all-loving Father. A Father, unlike any earthly father, Who was in total control of all things.

'Our Father is not having a breakdown because of unemployment in this country,' Ian declared with conviction. 'He is sitting on his throne saying, 'I can look after my own people. Everything is going according to plan. I see all – not all up to now, but all, past, present and future.'' Ian pointed out the many times we repeated, 'Thy will be done on earth as it is in heaven,' but rarely expected that to come about.

'Come to the Father in the name of Jesus and tell him you want his will done on earth as it is in heaven – and mean it,' he said. 'Is there sickness in heaven? Imagine getting eternally sick, for ever and ever with no hope of improvement? But, you may ask, how can God's will legally be done on earth now? Because Jesus Christ, a citizen of heaven, came to earth and brought heaven's ability with him. A man from another planet would have another planet's power. So Jesus came from heaven where he had access to all God's mighty power.'

Pauline sat listening and praying at the same time.

'Lord, do you think I should go forward for ministry?' She prayed silently, and the Lord Jesus assuring her of his access to his Father's power spoke clearly in her heart, 'I am the Lord that heals you.' 'Alright, Lord,' Pauline responded in the depths of her being, 'Alright. I trust you to heal this pain. I can't go on living like this any longer. I trust you to free me from it tonight.'

Making her way to the front she briefly told Ian her problem. Then she tells us what happened.

'Sit on that chair and put your legs out,' he told me and showed me how short one of my legs was compared with the other. 'When the Lord has finished with you you are going to be either shorter or taller, which do you prefer?' Ian asked with a smile.

'I didn't care one way or the other so simply lifted my hands in the air and thanked the Lord for what I believed he was going to do. And, as Ian prayed for me, I felt God's touch! This was no case of wishful thinking. God put me straight and I knew it. Getting to my feet I was unsteady and a bit off balance because God had levelled me up and I wasn't used to being on an even keel!

'Something happens inside when the Spirit of God heals a body after years of pain. It's incredible, exciting, awe-inspiring and wonderfully real. But as the days go on and the reality of the healing dawns on you then no one, not anyone in the world can convince you God is dead or doesn't care. My God took away the excrutiating pain that had been part of my life for years and I will praise him and thank him until the end of my days.'

Go and get that dog

Stewart Duke is a retired engineer who served as a captain in the army in World War II. He lives in the Medway Valley, east of London.

Apart from a very slight limp there is no evidence of his previous disabilities.

Stewart Duke stumbled wearily up the steep hill. Another few yards and he would have to stop and rest again. His good arm was supported by a stout walking stick, but the arm paralysed by a severe stroke had, somehow, to carry his few groceries. It was not more than half a mile from his third floor flat to the shops but Stewart had to set aside most of the morning to do his shopping.

Pausing to get his breath and rest, he saw a past acquaintance coming his way. That was too much. He turned into a shop doorway and stared unseeing into the window. It was so embarrassing to try to talk with his slurring, indistinct speech. Life was a trial and a lonely, difficult trial. So many times he had thought back over the years, never dreaming they would end like this.

He had finished the war able and healthy and had returned to set up home in the Medway area with 'the loveliest girl in the world.' She had been so proud of him in his Captain's uniform and life stretched ahead with all its opportunities. They had been so happy. He had fulfilled his working life as an engineer, and, although he and his wife had not had a family, they were perfectly content together.

As the years passed, however, Stewart developed a cough and it became obvious that he was becoming a very sick man. The outcome was that he was taken into hospital and had to have a cancerous lung removed. But things began to get back to normal and slowly health and strength returned. Then one day, Stewart had a shattering experience. Just as things were ticking over steadily, he had a disastrous stroke. His arm, his leg and his speech were all severely affected. And this time his troubles didn't go away. There had been times when he wondered why God had let him live, but at least he had his dear wife to care for him.

But there came a day when the most shattering blow of all hit him. It was like a nightmare. His beloved wife had an accident, developed emphysema and died. Why had she gone so quickly and he had been left to stumble around all alone?

Once on his own, Stewart had no choice but to set out on what seemed a marathon walk to the shops. The stairs down from the flat were bad enough, he was so afraid of falling. And then, once outside he set his will to cover a certain distance, rest, cover a few more yards and rest, and keep going somehow till he reached the shops. Then there was the difficulty of getting inside and the even greater problem of telling the assistant what it was he wanted to buy.

Now he was on the way back from one of those shopping trials which ended with the long haul back up the stairs to the refuge of his flat. A refuge, yes, but a lonely refuge punctuated with difficulties through his disabilities.

The brighter areas of Stewart's dark days were provided by his friends. They stood by him and did all they could to help him along. Some of them suggested that a dog would be company for him. They even told him of a breeder down on the coast at Rye who had two or three pups available. But what was the use? Stewart phoned her and had a talk, but it was out of the question. As he says, it was all he could do to get himself out and down the steps from his flat, and even worse to get himself back up again. How could he ever cope with a dog with its needs and its walks?

He told his friends it was a nice idea but he couldn't do it.

What he could do, however, was accompany a friend to the United Reformed Church not far from his home. Having always been a churchgoing man, it was nice to have someone to go with. When he didn't go there, he went to a Catholic church and made friends with the priest. Both churches were near enough for him to attend.

One day, both the priest and Stewart's other friend told him of a special meeting they were planning to attend. It was to be held in the United Reformed Church Hall but his friend the priest assured him it was very special and he would also be there. The speaker was to be a man Stewart had never heard of, one, Ian Andrews, and it was to be a healing meeting.

'They both urged me to go,' Stewart tells. 'But I didn't want to one bit. Going out at night with my disability was no pleasure so I can't say I was looking forward to it at all. However, my friend told me it would do me good and eventually I agreed to go.'

Having given his word, Stewart wouldn't have let his friend down so along he went on the special evening. The church hall was packed when he got there but he found one of the seats still vacant and sat down. And very soon the singing and atmosphere lifted his spirits and he began to really enjoy himself. When Ian Andrews got up to speak there was already a joy among the crowd present and a feeling of expectancy. The reading was not one Stewart had heard before. It came from Proverbs 30 vv. 18, 19 and was about four things that Solomon found very wonderful.

Ian spoke about the eagle, the first of the four things, and he began to explain the characteristics of the eagle and how it would crouch high up on a rock, listening for the sound of a rising current of air. Then he likened that picture of the eagle to the members of God's family listening for the wind of the Spirit of God.

'When that wind current comes,' Ian explained, 'All you need to do is soar up with praise and worship into the presence of God.' He turned to look round the crowded hall.

'When the wind of the Spirit is here, as I believe it is now,' Ian continued, 'You can get as close to God as you want to if you let your spirits rise with his Spirit.'

'I suggest everybody present seeks to rise now in praise and worship – you can be healed in this way, you can be delivered in this way, you can be baptised in the Holy Spirit as you rise up into the presence of God.'

Stewart had never heard anything like it before but he let himself reach out and respond and was filled with a feeling of elation.

Ian never did go on to the rest of his talk. The Spirit of God took over the meeting and Stewart was only one of many who was affected deep down in his being.

The meeting eventually ended and Stewart made his way to the door.

'Would you like me to walk you home?' It was his Catholic friend alongside him in the crowd.

'No. Thank you very much. No. I shall be quite alright.' Somehow it seemed unnecessary. He got outside without a problem and then, still elated and thinking about the service he walked home and up the stairs to his flat. Then it dawned on him. He hadn't had to rest all the way home! And, incredibly, he had walked straight up the twenty-eight stairs without a stop. It must be the result of the great feeling of elation that made him still feel like that eagle soaring upward in the sky.

Stewart went to bed relaxed, elated, the best he had felt for ages. He eagerly looked forward to being in church the next morning. Then, as he lay there feeling wonderful and thinking over all that had taken place that evening, a gentle voice seemed to say to him, 'Go and get that dog.' Get that dog, he thought. What an extraordinary thought to break in on the wonder he felt at his experience in the meeting. But there it was again, 'Go and get that dog.' Would God tell him something like that? It seemed such a silly thing even to think, but, over and over again he heard, 'Go and get that dog.'

Lying in bed thinking, thinking, thinking, Stewart remembered the way he strode home just like old times. He thought of the way he plodded straight up those twenty eight stairs. Dare he believe that God had touched him and restored the ravages of the stroke of two years before? If he had, then maybe he could after all look after a little dog.

It was Sunday when Stewart woke up so he had his bath and dressed for church. And it was true! His leg was restored. His arm was as good as new, and when he spoke to himself in the mirror, there was no slurring, no mumbling, he could speak clearly again. He could hardly wait to meet his friend at church and tell him what God had done for him.

Then, there it was again, right out of the blue and totally unexpected, 'Go and get that dog.' Well, he would. He would do just that. With a feeling of suppressed excitement, he packed up some sandwiches for himself, collected a few biscuits and a container of water for the pup, put some money in his pocket and he was off down the stairs.

With a great thankfulness welling up within him he knew with every step that God loved him, Stewart Duke. God had healed him. Here he was, getting in his car to drive without a problem all the way to Rye and back when twenty four hours before he had wondered whether he should try to drive any distance at all in his state.

On returning home with a delightful little black Scottie, the first thing on the agenda was a good sharp walk right round a local grassy area. And the joy and gratitude as it presented no problem at all!

Since that very special evening Stewart Duke has done a lot of deep thinking and come up with some profound and God-given wisdom. He has found that God heals today but also believes the devil will heal sometimes, but the big difference is that God's touch brings light and joy and an inability to keep quiet about his goodness. The devil, Stewart tells, may make your body well but inside you are in darkness.

Out of gratitude for God's healing in his own life, Stewart has faced ridicule on occasions when he shared his experience. But that doesn't deter him in the least. How can he keep quiet when he was so pitifully weak and now has no problem as he and his little dog go out five times each day together.

'I can tell you,' he says, 'I thank God every night for what he has done for me and for giving me back my strength again.'

God works to his time-table

Mrs Rita Roulund and her husband and family live in Viborg, Denmark, where her husband is a medical doctor. They attend the local Baptist church.

'We had been missionaries in Africa for six and a half years but returned to our home country of Denmark in 1972. All went well for me at first but in 1974 I began to feel a little off-colour physically and out of sorts in my spirit as well. There was nothing obviously wrong with me but somehow my energy had gone and left me like a limp rag. Walking became more and more of an effort, standing in a queue for more than a few minutes left me exhausted and even sitting up drained me and made me feel really ill. I tried hard to keep going for the sake of my husband and children but everything became an effort and even standing preparing a meal in the kitchen was too much for me.

'My symptoms pointed to a very low blood pressure and my husband, being a doctor, prescribed some tablets to put me right. For a time they really helped and my strength returned but the improvement only lasted for a short time and then I began to slide back into the terrible lethargy. So I took more tablets and drank frequent cups of strong coffee to keep me going. Mornings were terrible. I was utterly drained, then improved a little through the day, before being completely useless in the evenings.

'There was a time when our church was running a mission and one day everything seemed to go wrong for me. We had planned to attend the meeting in the evening and had invited friends to come back and have coffee with us. Like most other women this had spurred me on to give the house a good clean and make it nice for their visit. After all the housework I felt the need to tidy myself also so had a bath to freshen me up. But instead of feeling fresh and ready for the evening I felt totally exhausted. I had no choice but to tell my husband he must go on his own as I was too tired to accompany him. And it wasn't just tiredness from doing a good job, but utter weariness with dizziness and a rapid heart beat. My husband was reluctant to leave me but eventually he went by himself and promised to come back immediately the meeting ended to see how I was feeling.

'As soon as he left the house I lay down and tried to relax by watching the television. But all the time I was conscious of my heart beating much faster than normal and waves of dizziness kept sweeping over me. Added to that I was having real difficulty with my breathing. About 9.15 p.m. my husband returned and asked me if I would like to go with him for a cup of tea with some friends of ours. He obviously wanted to go and I very much wanted to please him so we stood discussing the idea in the kitchen while we prepared the children's sandwiches for the next day. As I stood there that terrible tiredness increased and I began to yawn nonstop until my husband told me to lie down straight away. I went through to my bed but very soon realised something was seriously wrong so called him to come quickly. Hurrying in, he looked at me and then fetched his sphygnomanometer and tried to take my blood pressure. But he couldn't get a reading as I was going into shock. Frankly at that moment I thought I was going to die and asked my husband if he thought I was dying. 'I don't know,' he told me and added, 'But if you can think at all, turn your thoughts toward Jesus.' Then he gave me a couple of injections and called the ambulance. While we waited I was suddenly very thirsty and had a cup of tea while my husband phoned some friends and asked them to pray for me. Much of the next hour or so is a blank to me but then I roused to find myself in the Intensive Care Unit of the medical ward in hospital. There, because of the injections my husband had given me at home, I was only put on a saline drip. But through the night many samples were taken and tests made to try to find out what was wrong with me. Nothing could be found and as I lay there I wondered how it was possible to feel so ill with nothing wrong with me! The staff moved me into another medical ward and took blood samples every four hours through the next day. There were more discussions and more doctors involved but they all shook their heads. So they took yet more samples and did even more tests and sent me home with some tablets – which I had tried before to no effect – telling me to come back when they knew the results of the tests. I was told they would send for me in a few days. We waited. Nothing happened. Eventually, when we phoned for the third time they admitted they had somehow lost the samples! To try and resolve the mystery of my weakness I was then asked to attend outpatients and see a senior medical officer. Even he was baffled and sent me on to a heart specialist in Aarhus who told us there was absolutely nothing wrong with my heart. The only slight irregularity that had come to light was an imbalance of the Potassium/Sodium ratio in my blood (Ka/Na balance) and there was nothing they could do to correct that anyway.

'So, where to go from there? The only positive decision we took at that time was that we would not involve the hospital any more.

'But my life was so limited. For some time I had not been able to live a normal life for even one day. I would struggle up in the morning and get dressed but then had to rest on a bed brought into our lounge for me. Breakfast was eaten lying down and then I lay there sleeping and resting until lunch time with the telephone beside me in case I needed it. My lunch consisted of an open sandwich which I would get up and make and take back and eat in bed, usually lying down. Then I would rest through the afternoon before getting up again to start cooking the dinner for the family. But I could only do a little at a time as I was only able to stand up for ten or fifteen minutes before collapsing in a faint.

'This went on for a couple of years day in and day out. During the summer my bed was moved outside into the sunshine and I acquired a lovely sun tan. Visitors would call and find me looking tanned and apparently in good health but then I would stand up for some reason and all the colour would drain out of my face leaving me looking like death warmed up. My doctor husband tried every way he knew to help me but it was all to no avail. He tried to contact doctors in other countries to ask their advice and I was put on one medicine after another but, far from making me feel better, I only felt worse than ever. When I felt well enough I would pass the time of day reading, mainly Christian books that were faith builders or Christian biographies.

'One day when my husband and I were talking and searching for an answer to my predicament I told him of the thoughts that had passed through my mind shortly before I had been rushed into hospital on that memorable evening. My attention had been drawn to the injunction in James 5 vv. 14, 15 where it says, 'Is any sick among you? Let him call for the elders of the church and let them pray over him, anointing him with oil in the name of the Lord: And the prayer of faith shall save the sick, and the Lord will raise him up, and if he has committed sins, they shall be forgiven him.' 'I wondered if we should ask our minister to come and anoint me with oil and pray for me,' I told my husband. 'But I never mentioned it because we don't normally do that sort of thing in our church.' My husband looked at me. 'Surely it is not too late to do that now, is it?' he said. So we called our minister and asked him if he would be willing to come. Straight away he said he was willing and that he had had a feeling I was to ask him to do that. He then asked if he could bring a few others with him and I agreed as long as it was only a few who really wanted to come of their own free will and who believed the teaching of James 5 vv. 14,15.

'A few days later it was all arranged and the minister and four or five members of the Church Council came to our home. I was excited and believed with all my heart that I would be healed so it was a great moment for me when they anointed me with oil and stood round and prayed for me. Of course I expected to be healed immediately and completely but God had other plans. There was no doubt that my condition improved in the following days but I was by no means as well as I had hoped to be. For some time I had had an oxygen cylinder under my bed so that I could put on the mask whenever I needed it. I had hoped this would now be a thing of the past but I was not able to do without it especially during the night when my condition was often very poor.

'It was now September 1978, two years and eight months since I had first gone into hospital. God had taught me much and quickened my faith to believe that he is healing people today and therefore I could believe him to heal me in his own good time. There was considerable interest in some meetings to be held in Give and in Silkeborg when an Englishman, Ian Andrews, was coming to speak with a special emphasis on healing. I would have loved to go but how could I? By now I was more or less bedridden and dependent on an oxygen cylinder so it was quite impossible to even consider such a project. One of my friends from our prayer group came to see me and told me she thought I should go anyway. But when I explained to her how ill I really was she promised she would ask to be prayed for on my behalf as it was not by choice that I was staying at home. The following evening, true to her word, she went forward and was prayed for in my place. The next day she phoned me but all she would say was, 'Expect great things.' I hardly had time to wonder what exactly she was meaning when the phone rang again. It was Pastor Svend Boysen from Give to speak to my husband. He was asking if he and Ian Andrews and Ian's wife, Rosemary, could come along and pray for me because Ian felt God had laid it on his heart that they should do so. Naturally we said, 'Yes,' with joy and with trembling! Was this God's timing?

'When they arrived I didn't know what to expect but it was all very gentle. For half an hour or more Ian sat and asked about our life both in Africa and here at home in Denmark. Then he went on to talk about the finished work of Jesus at Calvary and how this included my illness. Of course by now I knew this but as Ian said, 'Faith comes by hearing and hearing by the word of God.' So he talked again about the stripes that Jesus bore on our behalf and how the Bible tells us that 'by his stripes we were healed.' At last he said, 'I do not know the cause of your sickness, whether it was a witchdoctor in Africa who wanted to harm you or whether it is bio-chemical, or what it is. But it does not matter. The important thing is that I know the cure! It is the finished work of Jesus!' To this I answered, 'I fully believe that, but my problem at the moment is not disbelieving what Jesus can do but that I don't know whether I can receive what he has for me.' He wasn't worried. 'You will know in a minute,' he said, 'When we lay our hands on you.' They laid their hands on me and prayed. I didn't feel a thing but a great joy flooded my heart and I believed.

'As they left the house I watched them go. Then I turned to my bed and a great longing to get in and rest came over me. But I knew I must play my part so remained sitting in my chair. Turning to my husband I said, 'Well, now I am healed, I cannot very well go back to bed even though that is the only thing I feel like doing!' Wisely he said nothing.

'Next day when my husband took my blood pressure he found it had started to rise. Also I could feel things happening in my body. I could sit upright with no difficulty and then I began to perspire freely, so much so

I had to bathe and change my clothes several times a day. I didn't feel 100% fit at that time but at least I avoided going back to bed. On the Sunday afternoon my husband went over to another meeting at Give and while he was out I sat down on my bed and declared my faith. I said that whatever happened I was not going to lie on that bed again because Jesus had touched me to heal me. Then I resolutely dismantled the bed, washed the bed clothes – including the blankets – washed the floor under where the bed had stood and changed the furniture around in the room. Where the bed had been I placed a small table and three chairs and then my two youngest children, aged ten and eleven at the time, came and helped me carry the bed out of the room. Of course they asked me why I was making all these changes so I told them that Ian Andrews had prayed for me, and that Jesus had touched me and healed me so I would not be needing the bed any more.

'It was such a happy time. The children understood straight away and suggested we should make a cup of tea and enjoy ourselves sitting at the little table which stood where my bed had been. So that is what we did and it was the next step of faith that I was able to take. Ten days later, with my strength steadily returning, I went to visit some friends who lived quite near us and I was able to walk all the way there and back. Two weeks after my healing I attended church for the first time in a long while. But when we were invited to a silver wedding anniversary a few days later I stayed at home thinking it might be too much for me. I regretted my decision afterwards because my husband went on his own and met Hjorth Lange and told him about my steady healing. Hjorth said that some were healed instantly, others slowly but warned that if you lost your faith because the healing was taking place slowly, it was possible to lose your healing completely. Telling me this when he came home I made up my mind to believe for a total healing and was encouraged as my condition steadily improved. Two months later I was well enough to go to the Advent Service, and after three months I was able to go ice-skating! By Whitsun we went together on a trip to Norway.

'Now I have been well for a long time. God is faithful and we praise him for all he has done for us. We thank him, too, for his faithful servants who minister his blessing. So many times I had prayed for myself and got out of bed in stubborn self-will determined not to return to bed, but this is not the way. It has to be God and we cannot force his hand. He works according to his time-table and does all things well.'

Which leg was it?

Alistair Crane lives near Liverpool with his parents and sister, Felicity. He is a lively boy, full of energy and showing no signs of the physical disability which caused concern in his boyhood.

Alistair's parents, David and Hilary Crane, met at school and became friendly in their mid-teens. About a year before their friendship developed, Hilary made a very real commitment to Jesus Christ during a Church Army Crusade at the Anglican church she attended. From that early commitment she went on with the Lord and was very concerned that, as their friendship began to turn to love, David should have the same goal of putting Jesus first and central in his life.

David, for his part, had attended a Methodist church encouraged by his parents, but it was a matter of duty in those early days. But when he and Hilary started going out together, Hilary would seek to turn his thoughts to the things of God by asking, 'What do you think of this aspect of faith, and what do you think about that Christian teaching?' and David would reply very honestly, 'I've never really thought about any of those things.' At this his teenage friend would reply, 'Well, you ought to think about these things. They are important.'

Perhaps because of Hilary's persistent prayer and witness, God began to speak to David at a much deeper level. Particularly through their marriage, David began to realise that if his love for Hilary was so great, how much greater must the Lord's love be for him. So, when they moved from their home area of Leicester and began their married life in the North West, they regularly attended the local Anglican church.

Their first baby, a girl, came along with no problems and it was not long after Felicity's birth that her father had a real experience of God. Visiting some friends back in Leicester, David and Hilary were invited to a house-meeting. David tells us, 'We had never heard anything like it before. People were speaking in different languages; there was singing – with people clapping their hands and obviously enjoying this form of worship. Then someone spoke out a message from God. It was all completely new to us but obviously very real to those taking part. Then, as the meeting continued, the man in whose house we were meeting came over to me and spoke to the effect that I was going to minister to many. That is all I can remember as I had not expected anything like that, but what I do remember is what I felt when he spoke. A tremendous heat came over me and I felt as though all my sin drained away and left me feeling clean deep inside.'

This took place in 1972 and was a turning point in David's life. Any doubts he had had dissolved away, he knew he had been born again into God's family, and from then on he really began to go on with God. Now that he is an elder in a similar fellowship he looks back to that day as the time when God filled him with the Holy Spirit. But, knowing next to nothing about such things in 1972, he returned home fired up to become active in the Anglican church they attended.

Then a second child was on the way and after a perfectly normal pregnancy, a healthy boy came into the world. But there was one cloud in the sky. Owing to Alistair's position before birth, he was born with a wasted leg and a foot twisted round out of alignment. The doctors described it as a club foot, but as it was not severe, they gave hope that in time it could possibly be cured by physiotherapy. A physiotherapist was brought into the situation and for some months came daily to strap the foot in the correct position. Later the visits became monthly but, to hold the foot straight, Alistair had to wear a corrective boot in bed at night.

The condition in no way affected Alistair's ability to walk, in fact he was on his feet at eleven months, but it was obvious that there was a difference in his legs and feet. The right leg was normal, but the left leg had no muscle shaping in the calf, was very thin, and the twisted foot was a whole size smaller than the normal foot.

It was when Alistair was two and a half that the family went to an Easter conference with their friends from Leicester. It was a wonderful experience for them because the Spirit of God was very present at the conference and they saw people being healed as they watched. One day someone asked David and Hilary if they had thought of asking for prayer about Alistair's leg and they admitted that it had not occurred to them that they should do so. However, they spoke to one of the conference leaders and he advised them to wait, expectantly, and see what happened. So they took Alistair to the various services but no message came from God specifically for him. Finally on the last morning of the conference, at the last meeting, and at the end of that meeting, the leader they had approached asked Ian Andrews if he would pray with Alistair.

At that time believing for healing was so new to David and Hilary that when Ian asked them what they would like God to do for Alistair they hesitated. The doctors had assured them that the misalignment in Alistair's foot could be corrected but no promise had been made about the wasted calf muscle and the short foot. So this was what they asked God to do, to make the calf muscle develop and the foot grow in size.

David tells us, 'I had my eyes closed and wasn't looking when Ian prayed.' But Hilary was determined to watch because she didn't want to fool herself or anyone else. She tells us, 'Ian was holding Alistair's foot as he prayed and I watched as the thin wasted calf muscle filled out and took the shape of a normal lower leg. And judging by Ian's reaction, he felt the foot grow, too.' This was in fact later confirmed when Alistair's feet were measured for his next pair of new shoes. The foot had grown. It was still slightly shorter than the other foot, but no more so than with many other children's feet.

Back home again, Alistair went for his regular visit to the doctor who had previously suggested it might be necessary to correct the misalignment by surgery as it was not responding permanently to the physiotherapy treatment. This time, however, he examined the leg carefully and then turned to Hilary. 'I don't think there is any need to operate,' he told her, 'But the foot will have to be in plaster for a while to help correct it.' A plaster was applied and stayed on for about three months and after its removal the hospital visits became less frequent. Then came the day when Hilary took Alistair for what turned out to be the confirmation of God's complete healing. As before the doctor read Alistair's notes and then examined his legs. 'Ah,' he began, 'Now let me see. Which leg was it?' Hilary kept quiet as both legs and feet came under close scrutiny but deep down inside she was praising God because of the doctor's dilemma.

Now, several years later, David and Hilary are still full of praise that God answered their prayer and gave them exactly what they asked for. They had been so new to the healing power of God that they had asked for the impossible, leaving the doctors to correct that which came into the medically possible. But, as they have seen God heal many, many people, they have come to understand something of the greatness of his love. In the same circumstances today they would have asked for complete wholeness and know that that is what they would have been given because it is in the nature of God to do the miraculous and his desire to express himself by doing something creative.

One important side effect of Alistair's healing has been on their family life. They have only to glance at Alistair's perfectly formed calf muscle to be reminded that the great Almighty God cares for them down to the smallest detail. And this has been a real encouragement to them to pray for their children with believing, specific prayer. One result of this has been a lovely close family union, another, a living faith in all their lives as they move ahead in their walk with God.

In pain for forty years

Fred Tobin and his wife Vera live in Avon in the West of England. Although approaching retirement, Fred can look ahead with eagerness. He and his family have been through tragedy and sorrow but have now experienced the touch of God throughout their family.

' 'Won't you ever learn?' my mother asked as I trailed into the house with blood on my face and knees again. 'How many times have I told you boys not to race down the hill on your bicycles? One of these days one of you will kill yourself.' She bustled away to get supper for the eleven of us, Mum, Dad, seven boys and two girls.

'My brother and I looked at each other and pulled faces behind her back. It was the biggest thrill imaginable to pedal like mad from our house at the top of the long slope that ran right down to the coast, and then whizz round the corner at the bottom and hope to stay on! One of us was always crashing and my bike had been a write-off more than once. At fifteen I considered myself old enough to take care of myself like my three older brothers. If the three younger than I wanted to pamper themselves then that was their lookout. But I had to admit I did feel a bit odd that evening. I'd gone down the hill at what I considered a very reasonable speed earlier in the day but, on turning the corner, had run slap bang into a man pushing his bike. I landed in the road but considered it quite a minor crash as I was able to get up and remount my bike without much problem.

'But later that day I felt really ill and after a day or two, scared as well. Going to the toilet I had seen to my horror that I was passing blood in my water. Mum put me to bed and called the doctor and he decided I must have gone down with glandular fever. 'Keep him in bed a few days and he'll soon be all right,' he advised. But I wasn't all right. Stupidly I didn't tell anyone but as I lay in bed I had a most peculiar feeling inside, as if hot blood was dripping. If I'd only said something it might have saved a lot of trouble but instead I tried to convince myself I was imagining it. One thing was obvious to everyone and that was that my mid-teen appetite had deserted me. I couldn't eat a thing. Mother tried enticing me with all my favourite dishes but it was no good, I couldn't eat no matter how tasty it looked. So eventually, six weeks after the accident, I was sent to a hospital up in London.

'At the hospital it was just the same. I couldn't eat and lost so much weight that after a month or two I could loop my finger and thumb round my leg and move them up and down. Eventually after eight weeks of this I was taken to the operating theatre and there they found I had torn my kidney and ripped it out of place and they had to repair it and stitch it back in position. I lost a year out of life getting over that, a year that was punctuated many times each day with great globules of cod liver oil and malt! Whether it was just the injury or time that passed before the trouble was dealt with I don't know, but from that time for forty years I had recurring pain where I had originally felt the dripping-blood sensation.

'Well, life has to go on and the years passed and I married and we had a family of our own. Both our son and daughter married and for a time everything went smoothly. But our son had jumped into matrimony while very young and before many years he was home again with his little boy and a broken heart.

'One night, very late, there was a loud knock on our door. Outside stood a policeman and fear gripped me as he asked if Michael Tobin lived here. 'What is it?' I asked as Vera, my wife, came up behind me. 'There's been an accident.' How right he was. There had been a terrible,

terrible accident. We now live at the top of a long steep hill that runs down into Bath and Michael had been driving slowly up that hill on his own in a Dormobile Caravanette. Nearing the brow of the hill, a car had come over the hill top at high speed and smashed right into the driver's side of the Caravanette.

'With all the panic of such news we hurried to the hospital to find Michael in the Intensive Care Unit. As his father I was allowed in to see him but there were two patients in the Unit and Michael was so severely injured I didn't know which one he was. It turned out that his leg was fractured in five places, his arm in two, he had a great tear over his eyes and the windscreen wiper had embedded itself in his neck.

'So began five years of hospital treatment, physiotherapy, rehabilitation and the like and the end result was that Michael wore a shoe built up more than an inch to level him up. As if this wasn't enough, our daughter's marriage also came unstuck and one night we were in the house all together with our bitterness and grievances and it blew up into a real family row. There was nothing going right with us and Michael in particular felt he had taken all he could bear. Next morning Vera went downstairs and he was gone. She came and told me and immediately we both thought the worst had happened. Sick with fear, I dressed and half ran, half walked along the canal bank at the bottom of our garden, dreading to see any sign of our son and yet desperate to find him. I was away some time as I felt compelled to check the bridge over the railway in case he had gone there. Stumbling home a broken, frightened man, it turned out he had hobbled to town on his crutches to get out of the four walls. The sorrow and tension and tragedy we were living in did nothing to help my own condition and the pain grew steadily worse. I found I couldn't sit still for any length of time but neither could I get back up on my feet the pain was so severe. To be honest, there didn't seem a great deal of point to life at all.

Looking back now, that must have been the deepest part of the valley we had to travel through. From then on, unnoticeably at first, things began to change. To enrich his restricted life, Michael joined a choir, and there he became friendly with a girl who eventually invited him to a fellowship of Christians. Of course we knew little about this. What we did know was that one night Vera and I were sleeping peacefully when there was a noise down below, then footsteps running up the stairs and our door burst open.

'Mum, something's happened. Both my legs are the same length!' It was Michael, so excited he could hardly contain himself. 'A man came to the fellowship tonight, and Mum, he prayed for me and my short leg grew to the right length again.'

'He went on but I was so hard headed at the time I was annoyed at being woken, and anyway, what was all this about legs growing. All I wanted was to be left alone to get a good night's sleep. But my wife caught the thrill of it all and was up and asking questions and as excited as Michael. Later when things quietened down a bit she lay thinking. Michael said it was Jesus who had done this miracle for her son. Well, if Jesus had done that, there must be something she should do. Into her thoughts flashed a verse of scripture, 'Repent, and be baptised.' That was what she had better do. So she repented as best she knew how and the next day, coupled with the excitement of taking Michael's shoes to have the built up heel ripped off, she made enquiries about being baptised. Meanwhile I felt like a table tennis ball being batted around. I couldn't believe Michael was healed. Even when I saw with my own eyes and watched him dig out a pair of old shoes to go to the doctor. It was all too amazing. Then my wife had gone religious and the climax to that came at six o'clock the next Saturday morning. At that early hour she plucked up courage to tell me she was going to be baptised the next day. But, more than that, she told me we had always done everything together so I was to be baptised as well! So on the Sunday, she was happily baptised, and, after I had talked my way through half a dozen questions about my faith in God, I was also baptised, not fully aware of what I was doing. But God knew! The next morning I woke with such a hunger for the things of God I had a gap a mile wide that desperately needed filling by God. There was just one big problem. I could not understand how Jesus could possibly have died for me personally. I had to wait six months before that became clear to me.

'The Sunday before Christmas, 1975, I wandered into the living room just as the film Alamo, a Western, was starting. With nothing particular to do I sat down to watch it and in many ways it was typical Western drama. It was about the Americans and Mexicans fighting over Texas with the usual ambushes, chases and shooting. But the climax of the film centred on a fort in which was a real tough bunch of army men. Somehow they were supposed to reorganise their troops to face an attack from about five thousand Mexicans surrounding the fort. It was all very dramatic and centred on the officer in charge of the garrison of American soldiers who was seeking to encourage and challenge his men to do their best. However, one officer had a disagreement with the officer in charge and declared that he and his men were going to break out in the morning and get away. When morning came, sure enough, that particular officer and the men under him were mounted and ready to break out when the officer changed his mind and decided to stay, leaving his men to please themselves. By this time I was deeply involved in the story and thought with concern, 'He's going to give up his life because everyone in the fort will be killed.' As I thought this an amazing thing happened. I actually heard a voice say, 'Greater love has no man than this that he lay down his life for his friends.' And as I heard this I had a vision of the Cross, shining brilliantly.

Suddenly I knew that Jesus had died for me and that he did it because he loved me. I can't explain it or enlarge on it or anything, I just knew.

'Church attendance had been a joy before this but now it was all I wanted to do. But there was one drawback. The pain inside me was becoming so severe I could scarcely bear it, and getting up and down in church was agony. There were times when I went to the Communion rail and wondered if I would be able to get back on my feet again. At home it was the same and Vera became quite adept at rolling me out of bed and heaving me out of chairs. Obviously something would have to be done but I dreaded going to the doctor. When I'd almost made up my mind to make an appointment I would start thinking of all I went through as a lad and then I'd funk it and determine to carry on a bit longer. I was only afraid someone would complain about my work and I would be fired.

'Just as things were coming to a head physically we heard Ian Andrews was coming to speak at a special meeting. By now we were attending two Fellowships, our own Anglican church and going to every meeting in a radius of ten miles that we could fit in. Both Vera and I felt we had so much leeway to make up that we would go anywhere to learn more.

'To be sure of a good seat we arrived half an hour before the meeting was due to begin. We always did this although it meant an extra half hour for me to fidget and wriggle to try and ease my pain. I don't know what we expected, but when Ian Andrews got up to speak it was the first we knew it was to be a healing meeting. As soon as he began he caught our attention because he was explaining the difference between a Christian being healed by Jesus and a non-Christian being healed by Jesus. He told us that when a non-believer hears about God's ability to heal he can pooh-pooh the whole thing and deny that it can happen. So, very often God will heal the non-believer to prove that Jesus Christ is Lord and does what he says he can do. But with the believer it is different. When a believer goes to a healing meeting, Ian told us, he needs to prove to God that Jesus Christ is Lord of his life. It is not a matter of going into God's salesroom and slapping down a few coins of faith and expecting to be handed healing and health in exchange. The believer needs to come in a serious frame of mind and submitted to the Lordship of Christ. This means putting his own thoughts about the situation away and thinking God's thoughts about his or her condition. Taking us through verses about healing Ian explained that, although we might have something physically wrong, the truth is that the stripes Jesus suffered at the whipping post, he suffered so that we can be healed and live in health. He quoted Proverbs 23 verse 23, 'you have to buy the truth and sell it not,' meaning that we need to buy what God has said with the price of making him our Lord and then God will watch over his word to perform it and the Holy Spirit will come and glorify God by healing the sufferer.

'All this made a lot of sense to me and spoke to my heart. I guess we had come into contact with Jesus Christ so late in life that it was all or nothing, his Lordship or nothing at all, we certainly were not interested in simply being religious. By the time Ian was calling people out and praying for them my heart must have been ready to believe and submit and go along with all that had been said because, as he prayed, I felt myself getting a feeling of increasing warmth in the area where I had such a lot of pain. I hadn't given a thought to my own problem until then, but as the warmth increased I knew without a doubt that God was healing me after all those years. When Ian asked if anyone felt they were being healed I responded at once, saying I was being healed from pains I had had for years. Later on he advised me to keep claiming my healing and that was a great help because during the following few days I got the occasional niggle but it went again as soon as I declared with conviction, 'Through

Jesus' stripes I have been healed.'

'But that wasn't the only way God showed his love for me that evening. Several times Ian mentioned that there was someone present with haemorrhoids and if the person concerned would go forward for prayer God would heal them. Not being medically minded in any way I wasn't sure what haemorrhoids were and, anyway, I was so excited about what was going on inside me, my attention was diverted. But near the end of the meeting I leaned over to Vera and asked her if haemorrhoids and piles were the same thing! When she told me they were I got to my feet and went forward for prayer and my wonderful Lord Jesus healed me from that problem as well!

'From that day to this we never stop talking about the love God has for us. That Jesus died to save us from our sins is the biggest miracle of all, but the fact that he cares about our health and strength and everyday lives is a wonderful discovery to make. We were an ordinary family like countless other families and yet God knew our needs and met them beyond anything we could hope for. He not only healed me that night, but in his love he has also healed our daughter's marriage and she and her husband and two children have all come to know Jesus as Saviour and Lord of their lives as well. Now we are an ordinary family blessed in an extraordinary way that is available to anyone who dares to believe God is really God, alive and powerful and longing to show his love for us.'

My sickness was bigger than my God

Mrs Joan Brett is the wife of a minister on the south coast of England. They and their sons face all the joys and pressures of church leadership but that is no longer a problem to Joan.

In a small house in East Ham, East London, some forty five years ago, a little girl of eight lay in bed listening. Then, as the stairs creaked under the heavy steps of her parents coming up to bed, she shrank down under the bed clothes and lay motionless, pretending to be asleep. It seemed so unfair that she had to sleep in the same room with them but there was nowhere else for her to go. The door opened and they came in, her mother fussing and anxious and her father angry and frustrated. It was the same every night. A disagreement in quiet voices became an argument that increased in volume. And, tucked under her bed clothes Joan tensed up until she could hardly breathe and felt as if her chest was clamped in steel bands.

Eventually the day arrived when Joan had a room of her own, but by then it was too late. The breathlessness and tension was so established that it came on in the day time as well as during the night. One day she told her mother she couldn't breathe but, of course she could breathe or she wouldn't be standing there. She was sharply told not to be silly and the problem brushed aside. That was the last time Joan sought help at home. In fact it was many years later when undergoing a routine medical check that the suggestion was made that the cause of her attacks of tension could result from these childhood fears.

As the one suffering the attacks there didn't seem rhyme or reason for their occurrence or absence. Evacuation during the war, which caused nervous problems to many, gave Joan a happy time with total freedom from breathlessness but, once home again, the trouble returned. In fact one day in her late teens Joan set off for the station to catch a train to work and was suddenly so short of breath and felt so ill she had to return home.

Poor Joan. A broken leg or a cut finger she could understand, but this? When everyone else was normal and chatting together, why was she feeling as if some great force was strangling her? A terrible despondency and despair began to fill her as she couldn't understand and couldn't break free. Was no one able to help her?

In her twenties plans were made for a two year stay in Canada and as the time drew near for her to go Joan suffered a terrible attack and almost called off the trip. But then, instead of being unable to cope, she adjusted, lost all her symptoms and had a thoroughly happy time.

On her return, however, it was the same old story all over again. In time marriage loomed on the horizon with further problems and a fiancé not sure of what he was taking on. But then a new hope of release came to Joan's attention. Up and down the country God was moving in a way not seen on a large scale for many years. Both churchgoers and non-churchgoers were being drawn into meetings where the Holy Spirit was touching people's lives both physically and spiritually in the way Jesus himself did when he lived on earth. Perhaps Joan would find release in this way?

So followed a life which swung from guilt at having to take tablets to cope with the bad attacks to hope on hearing of another healing meeting and finally disappointment when nothing helped. But Joan was not one to give up. There had to be an answer somewhere.

It was in this frame of mind that Joan joined the healing line at a Catholic church not far from home. Surely this time God would meet her need? But no. With real disappointment she left the church untouched and feeling lonely and in need of real fellowship. Within a day or so, she and her husband went to a Christian bookshop on a routine shopping trip when a notice in the shop caught Joan's eye. Ian Andrews was speaking locally that very week. Putting aside any thought of healing for Joan they made up their minds to go and enjoy the teaching and fellowship. They did invite an elderly blind lady from their congregation to go with them but, at the last minute, she was unable to go and so Joan and David found themselves settling down to join with the large crowd who came along to the church in Southport. It was so good to be on the receiving end of Bible teaching for a change.

After a time of worship and praise Ian began to speak about blind Bartimeus and David thought how good it would be for Joan to receive ministry by proxy for the old lady unable to accompany them. But for Joan the whole story of Bartimeus became new and spoke to her heart as it had never done before. As Ian brought the story to life he pointed out that Bartimeus was faced with a clear cut choice. No doubt he had sat with his beggar's cloak and beggar's bowl for many a day, listening to the feet passing and catching snatches of conversation. He had heard of this man, Jesus and amazing stories of people being made well and even receiving their sight after years of blindness.

Then came the day when he sensed a ripple of excitement in the crowd. Straining to hear more he heard that name, Jesus, again and soon he realised that Jesus was coming along and would pass close by. The choice before him was to either sit there, despised and remaining in his need or to shout out loud enough to attract Jesus' attention. In his condition the choice did not take long to make, this could be his only chance and, anyway, what did he have to lose? With his heart beating fast, he waited as he heard the crowd approach and then in a loud voice he cried out. But what was this? Surely Jesus was son of Joseph the carpenter of Nazareth? But Bartimeus cried out, 'Jesus, son of David, have mercy on me.' Somehow the blind, despised nobody knew with certainty who Jesus really was. The disciples and the crowd around were not a bit impressed and tried to silence him but Bartimeus was not to be silenced. Again he shouted at the top of his voice, 'Son of David, have mercy on me.'

Engulfed in the throng around him, Jesus heard that cry and called Bartimeus to him. And, as the crowd passed the message to Bartimeus he leaped up with faith and threw off his coat, the symbol of his blindness and pushed through the crowd to Jesus.

Bringing a message to instil faith in the hearts of his listeners Ian drew a parallel between Bartimeus and those who hear the story today.

'Everyone who comes into the presence of Jesus today is free to sit tight and remain in need or reach out to Jesus who wishes to meet our needs,' he said and went on.

'If people will recognise who Jesus really is, they will come with confidence to meet with him.'

'But,' Ian explained, 'perhaps the greatest step of faith Bartimeus took was to throw off his symbolic coat showing the world he was blind, and step out with the mind and faith of a seeing man who has left the past behind?

That step changed everything for Bartimeus Once Jesus responded to his call, the very people who had tried to quieten him and keep him in the background now jostled him to the front of the crowd with words of encouragement. And the human heart is the same today. The thought of attending a healing service brings cries of protest even from friends, as Joan knew well. How many times had she been advised to accept her problem and resign herself to her condition. After all, if God is God, surely he could heal her if he wanted to without her making a fool of herself over and over again.

But Joan pushed such thoughts away and listened intently to everything Ian was saying. One sentence in particular really spoke to her. Ian was pointing out how easily Bartimeus could have settled for his blindness and not given Jesus the opportunity of faith which he needed. Then looking out over the crowd Ian said, 'Unfortunately, some of us have made our sicknesses bigger than our God.' That was it. Joan knew in a flash, that was what she had done.

From that moment Joan's faith began to rise and a feeling of expectancy grew inside her. By the time Ian called for people to come forward for healing she was ready and eager and almost healed of the tension that had niggled at her even as she listened. Every previous time she had gone forward she had been prayed for for healing, but, on telling Ian her problem the Lord revealed to him this was not a case for healing but that a spirit of tension had been troubling Joan all down the years. With authority, Ian commanded the spirit to 'Go!' and the tension was broken. And as so often happens, the power of the Holy Spirit gently knocked Joan to the ground as he worked in her. But only for a moment. Getting to her feet she turned to David, standing beside her. 'I'm healed!' she burst out. But David already knew that by the peace and joy in her face.

Forty five years of those dreadful attacks and now Joan was free. No wonder she sang and her step was light. Everything was going to be so different from now on. Or was it?

Two days after she had returned home so elated, Joan and David and two young people from the church got out the car and packed the boot full of Christmas toys to take to a nearby Children's Home. They set off, talking and laughing together when suddenly Joan felt that dreadful tension begin in her chest. And it got tighter and tighter until she could hardly breathe. It was a vicious attack from Satan to regain his old home. For a moment Joan didn't know what to do. She didn't want to frighten the young people and, anyway, she could scarcely speak. Then, quite suddenly she realised that the devil hates to be defeated and to see God's children living in victory.

As she sat there, deep within her she rebuked Satan in the name of Jesus just as earnestly as she knew how. And, of course, he had to leave. She was free again. It happened again as she went to bed that night. This time David joined in the battle and, using the strong name of Jesus against the enemy, commanded him to leave.

But Joan was not to be beaten. She had tasted freedom and knew it was her right as a child of God. When the enemy tried another tactic and woke her in the night gasping for breath, she was ready. As far as she was concerned he could try again and again but he could not win. The battle had already been won on her behalf by Jesus. Before long the devil realised he was defeated so finally gave up.

Today, with the battles finished long ago, Joan, relaxed and happy, will tell anyone who asks her,

'It's great. I'm free. Thank you, Lord. It's so wonderful.'

I praised the Lord with great joy

Sven Frohm lives in Northern Sweden. At the time of his accident he was a forestry worker but had to change to lighter work and became a car salesman.

'It was in the 1950s and, as usual in a Swedish winter, it was bitterly cold. But I was used to it and went off to work in the forest like any other day. Even in subzero temperatures it is hot work felling trees. Soon the eerie silence of the snow covered mountainside was ringing with the strike of the axe and roar of the mechanical saw. Every so often there was a shout of warning, followed by the whine of the falling tree as it crashed through neighbouring branches and thudded to the ground. The work was hard but healthy and I found it very satisfying. As a young man in my twenties the physical exertion broadened the shoulders, swelled the muscles and made me feel every inch a man. Even so there were dangers and over confidence led to more than one severe injury. But I was careful. I had a lovely wife and a young son and, anyway, I knew how to take care of myself.

'Then, that day the unexpected happened. I was working on a steep mountain side, high up where the ground was frozen solid when, suddenly, I slipped. I grabbed to catch something to stop myself but it was too late. Before I knew what was happening I was sliding on my back down the steep slope. Gaining speed rapidly I seemed to bounce from one tree stump to another to a rock to a tree stump, striking the base of my spine against each projection. On and on I went, wondering if I would ever stop and, when eventually I was flung into the snow at the bottom of the slope I felt bruised and breathless and broken. As it happened, when I felt able to move, I found each part of me worked alright and nothing was apparently broken. So, grateful to God, I went back to work and kept my job for several years although I had continuous pain at the base of my spine which had taken the most punishment.

'It was not until a few years had passed and the pain was so severe I could no longer do heavy work that I eventually went to the doctor for advice. He sent me for an X-ray and it was discovered that gristle had formed over the coccyx at the base of my spine and this was the cause of the pain. There was little that could be done to help me but it was suggested that I should change my work and look for a lighter job with less physical demand. It seemed to be the only way ahead so I gave the idea much thought and eventually was able to find a job as a car salesman. Of course, the pain continued to trouble me but it was less of a problem than it had been in forestry work.

'By this time the doctor had me under his care and when I received my next call up to do a month's military service, he sent a letter to the military headquarters stating that I was unable to carry my own knapsack and so on owing to a back injury. This brought matters to a head because, although I was freed from further military service, at the same time I was taken to an orthopaedic clinic in Härnösand in order to undergo an operation. However, the hospital doctor examined me thoroughly and after taking more X-rays of my back his verdict was that it was advisable not to operate as he feared it might leave me disabled. The letter from the orthopaedic clinic to my own doctor briefly stated: 'Coccyx pushed sideways – causing the pain.' That was all. There was no treatment suggested, no recommendation for operation and no hope of any improvement. I was going to have to learn to live with pain for the rest of my life. Down through the years I have used painkillers in the form of suppositories and coped as best I could, but never was the hope of recovery presented to me.

'Then, one day in November 1980, the telephone rang. It was my son phoning from his home in Malmö. He was inviting me to a conference organised by 'Jutatorpet' to be held in Jönköping. Malmö is six hundred and sixty miles from my home and Jönköping only one hundred and fifty miles less to travel but we see so little of each other that I promised to meet him at the conference. Knowing the problem such a long journey would be to me I told him I would travel by plane cutting the journey to a fraction of the time. By the time I got in touch with the airline I was eagerly looking forward to the trip but I was to be disappointed. The flights were fully booked and there was no hope of my getting a seat in time to keep my promise to my son. But I knew he had been so pleased when I agreed to go that I didn't want to back out now. So, reluctantly, I found myself on the overnight train trying to snatch a few hours sleep in a sleeping compartment.

'By 9 o'clock next morning when the train drew in to Jönköping station the pain in my back was very bad. There was nothing that could be done about it so I said nothing when I met my son. Together we went along to the conference in time for the morning Bible study at 11 o'clock. The seating was hardly luxurious – wooden seats had been set out for us to sit on, but I managed to keep quiet and stuck it through both the morning and afternoon sessions. However, when it came time to go and eat it was obvious that I could hardly walk. Of course my son noticed this at once and realised an evening meeting would be just about impossible for me. This was disappointing for both of us but particularly so because Ian Andrews from England was to speak that evening. 'It would really be a shame if you couldn't attend tonight,' my son said. 'The Holy Spirit is using this man Ian

Andrews in healing. Jesus comes into the meeting and heals people from their sicknesses and wonderful things happen.'

'We talked it out and by 7 o'clock I had decided to go along. To help me my son arranged for me to have an armchair and that was a big improvement. In fact when the meeting began and then Ian Andrews began to speak, at first I didn't find it too hard to sit. But as time went by I began to fidget more and more. There I was with a comfortable armchair and yet hardly able to sit still while about two thousand others sat on those hard wooden seats and listened in wrapt attention and obviously no discomfort.

'Early on in Ian's message he encouraged all those with various sicknesses to reach out and ask Jesus to heal them no matter what was wrong. I prayed simply and earnestly, 'Yes, dear Jesus, please heal my back.' But having said it I thought no more about it because, frankly, I didn't believe that Jesus would pay any special attention to me. Like many people I thought miracles could happen to someone else but not to me personally.

'But then Ian Andrews began to say that Jesus was in the meeting, walking between the rows and healing people from their sicknesses. This was getting exciting! Suddenly Ian began pointing toward various parts of the hall and saying that the Holy Spirit was upon this person and that person and was healing them of heart disease, psoriasis and other sicknesses. Then pointing in my direction he said, 'The man who has a pain in his back, the Spirit is on you right now and Jesus is healing you!' 'That's you, Dad. Hallelujah!' my son said at once and then I became aware that something was happening to me. It's difficult to describe but I felt as if someone were using a typewriter on the part of my back that had been damaged. It was exactly like someone pressing a lot of buttons and I sat there in awe, hardly daring to believe that I was feeling the touch of God healing my back.

'After years of pain it is hard to believe that in a moment it can all be a thing of the past. So my first thought was to try it out and see if it really could be true! Getting up I walked past all the people to the exit at the back of the hall. Then, outside the main auditorium, I walked right down the stairs, then back up them again and went back to my place and sat down. 'Jesus has healed me!' I said to my son. 'I have no pain any more.' What joy. What an experience.

'Now, after twenty-five years, I am able once more to shovel the snow! And what is more I enjoy it so much I go and shovel snow for my neighbours as well. Snow was such a problem to me before Jesus healed me. Now I look on it as a gift from God.

'At the end of the service that memorable evening a film was shown about Jesus of Nazareth. It began at 11.00 p.m. and lasted for two hours. Knowing what Jesus had done for me I told my son I was intending to see the film and that I would sit on a wooden chair. The joy on his face was for all to see as I sat through the two hours with no difficulty.

'One year after Jesus healed me I had an interesting experience. I was travelling by train to Stockholm and got talking to a man who didn't believe in God. He told me he couldn't believe without proof so I told him of the accident I had in the forest, of how the X-rays had caused the doctors to tell me I should change my work and how, twenty-five years later, God had completely healed me. I quoted him Mark 16: 17, 18, 'these signs shall follow them that believe . . . they shall lay hands on the sick and they shall recover.' Not convinced, he asked me if I had been X-rayed since I had had this experience, so that I had proof of my healing. I assured him that I needed no further proof beyond the fact that I was well and strong whereas I had been in pain for twenty-five years. But I also told him that I was due to go in to hospital for spinal X-rays the following week for a check up.

'So, on 13th November 1981, just one year after my healing, I arrived at Sundsvall hospital. I had been having an inflammation in my right arm and the X-rays were to investigate the cause of this trouble. Everything was very straightforward. I went along to the X-ray department and, when my turn came, the radiographer took seven pictures of my spine. I was told to wait outside while they were processed and examined and was then called back in by the lady doctor in charge. She said she wanted to talk to me. Naturally I assumed the X-rays hadn't developed properly and that there were to be one or two repeats. But no. When I entered this lady doctor said she wanted to know when I had had the operation on my back as there was no record of it in my medical notes. I told her I had not undergone an operation on my back by any human doctor. But she didn't understand my meaning. 'No, seriously,' she said. 'Tell me. You have had an operation, haven't you?' I assured her I had not, but then I realised this was the proof that my friend on the train had wanted. Certainly no human surgeon had dared to operate, but the Lord, my Creator and Great Physician, had not only performed a delicate operation successfully, but there was actually a mark at the base of my spine where he had done this miracle of healing. I was so happy about it I left the hospital praising the Lord with great joy. How I thank God that, through his grace, I am able to be one of his children.'

It had to be God

Mrs Ruth Norton has lived in the south east of England for several years after spending most of her life in Zambia. She is of South African origin but left there at twenty-one years of age to live and work with Africans whom she dearly loves.

''What ever is the matter with me?' I thought for the umpteenth time as I dragged myself off to the office. I ran an import company in Zambia and found my work challenging and interesting. With a real love for the African people and no problem relating to them, I was in my element running the company I owned. But something was amiss. I can only describe my feeling as absolutely 'yuk' and deadly weary. It had to be dealt with so off I went to my doctor who returned the verdict of hepatitis. But normally hepatitis, although making you feel deadly ill at its worst, does slowly begin to respond to treatment. I didn't. For months I had to force myself to do anything and, on returning home from work, I collapsed on the bed totally exhausted. Far from improving, my condition steadily deteriorated until one Friday morning I reached the end of my resources. 'It's no good,' I told my husband. 'I can't go to work. I'm through.' The doctors were still convinced it was hepatitis until one morning things came to a crisis. I'd noticed a peculiar smell that came from me and it began to worry me. There's nothing disgusts me more than being dirty and this smell wouldn't go away. So that morning I asked my husband if he would help me have a bath to get rid of it.

'Before bathing I'd noticed I was passing blood when on the toilet but somehow I'd not bothered about it. But, when I sat down in the bath it was as if a reservoir burst and blood poured from me. The details of the next hours elude me but the ambulance was called and a dear friend came rushing to help in every way she could. Her son was about to go to play rugby football, but he went out of his way to call at our local church, told them what had happened and asked them to pray for me. He even wrote a note, underlining his request and asking for prayer from as many as could be contacted.

'Meanwhile his mother, Joan Campbell, travelled in the ambulance with me to Luanshya Hospital at Ndola. She and the nurse hung over me as I went a dreadful colour and the journey seemed to go on for ever. Joan, my friend, kept praying all the way while the nurse repeated over and over, 'Is she still alive? Is she still alive?'! I remember nothing about the journey at all.

'There was no point in my friend waiting around so she left me there and went to the church that evening to join in prayer for me. While there, someone crept up to her and asked her to come out and she felt sure she was to hear that I had died. But no. As gently as possible she was informed that her dear son who had left the prayer request for me, had collided with a young man his own age on the rugger field and he was the one who had died. What a test of faith. But what a lovely last act, to go out of his way to ask for prayer on my behalf before going himself to be with the Lord.

'For my part at the hospital, my heart was failing, presumably due to the heavy haemorrhage I'd had. But, sometime in the night, I regained consciousness, opened my eyes and there sitting on my bed was one of the doctors. This dear man was a Christian and as soon as he saw I was looking at him he asked, 'Would you like me to pray with you?' I gave a little nod and he prayed with me very simply. But my breathing was terrible and he asked me how long it had been so bad but I was too weak to speak. Then he suggested calling my husband, but as he wasn't very well himself I managed a whispered, 'No.' I was losing consciousness again when I heard him tell the nurse, 'I'll stay with her because she won't make it through the night.'

'But God had another plan. He heard the volume of prayer that went up and he prompted the doctor to order blood transfusion and the next morning I woke again and continued to pick up as I received six pints of healthy blood. One week later, contrary to all expectations, I was discharged from hospital. I was not fully aware of how unexpected this was until I went for a check up and was told – this time by a non-Christian doctor – 'Mrs Norton, you have leukemia. We never expected you to leave hospital alive and really can't understand it.' But I did leave hospital and I felt much better, but I was not what I would call completely well. Although I lived in Zambia for several more years, I found the heat a great problem. I was always hot. Even when other people wrapped up and especially when I came over to England, I would see people in heavy sweaters and extra jackets, and I was trotting around in a cotton dress and still hot! Also I needed air all the time. It was most odd. I would be in a room with a lot of people and wasn't claustrophobic but would have to go out to get some air. Of course there was air in the room, but it had to be fresh and preferably moving for me to feel able to stay. And then there was tiredness. I could do so much and that was it, I ran out of energy and had no choice but to stop.

'Meanwhile the time was approaching when we should think seriously about retirement. We bought a house in Zambia for this purpose because that was home and that was where our hearts were. We were involved in the local church and with the missions working in Zambia and were very happy. But there were troubles around us and we ourselves had several bad robberies which spoiled everything. Instead of being a joy, our home became more like a fortress and with our children grown up and moved away, we were on our own. Then our thoughts turned to South Africa where I was born and brought up. Twice we went down there to buy a house and on the first of these visits we arrived on a Friday and made an appointment with an estate agent to see a house the following Monday. We had the money and everything seemed straight forward. Of course there was a Sunday before the day we had arranged to see over the house. So on the Sunday morning we agreed together that we would obey whatever the Lord told us to do in church that morning. We had many dear Christian friends in that town and they were keen for us to stay but that wasn't to be the deciding factor. We wanted to be where God wanted us to be. Off we went to church and what did the minister preach on but the Good Samaritan, stressing how easy it is to go over the road to new pastures and leave a necessary work behind! That was it. Back we went to Zambia for another period there. Some time later we tried again to find a house in South Africa but none of the places we looked at was right.

'Eventually, my friend Joan and her husband came over to England, their homeland, on holiday and something prompted me to write to her about property. Her reply amused us both. She put, 'Listen, my husband says I'm not to interfere with your affairs any longer – but here are lists of houses for sale in England!' This could only be God. I had spent one short holiday in England years earlier and didn't know it at all, but here I was finding out about houses thousands of miles from both home and roots. What is more, one house seemed to be the very one for us. But we didn't have the means in England to buy it. However, nothing daunted, I wrote a private letter to the owner with a suggestion. It went something like this. '. . . I don't mean to insult you or anything but we only have such and such a sum available but want to buy your house. I'm not wanting to knock down the price you are asking, can you wait while I negotiate a bridging loan?' Back came a letter, '. . . if you can get a bridging loan, the house won't go to anyone else.' So far so good, but now what? It was clearly a time for God to demonstrate his will for us. I decided there was nothing to lose so, almost with tongue in cheek wrote to the manager of Barclay's Bank who, of course, didn't know me from a bar of soap! We had in that bank the princely sum of £200. Well, we wrote him and told him our position, explaining that we had money in South Africa, that it would not be released for so long but we wanted a bridging loan. 'Thank you very much!' Surprise! Surprise! He wrote back to say, 'Yes.' So we had a bridging loan from someone we had never met to buy a house we had never seen in a country we had hardly visited. As I say, it had to be God.

'Not long afterwards we came over to England and went up to see the Bank Manager to thank him. He told us then that he hadn't known what to do when he received my letter as it was the most peculiar letter he had ever received.

'So we bought the house, lived in it a while and then returned to Zambia where I was keen to do relief work. It all seemed very odd at the time as we had no ties here and were deeply immersed in Africa in every way. But eventually, as we had this house, I came over on my own to stay for a time leaving my husband in Africa. One night I went up to bed and fell asleep, but during the night the Lord woke me and somehow told me very clearly that it was he who had brought me to England and he didn't want me to go back to Africa. Again, it had to be God because Africa was my life and my love. But he went on to impress upon me that my ministry was to be one of intercession – of earnest prayer for people and countries and situations. And particularly for Britain. Well, there is no point arguing with Almighty God so my husband came over and here we are.

'But I was still not well. I was still too hot and too weary and in need of 'air'! The prayer that dramatic night in the mid-seventies had certainly resulted in a remission and a remarkable remission, but the leukemia was always in the background and debilitating.

'With the commission from the Lord to pray, I became involved with the Lydia prayer groups. These are groups of ladies scattered all over Britain who had also been called to pray, in particular for this country. And it was to be my privilege to be involved, with thousands of other ladies, in this vital work. One day when I was attending a Lydia prayer meeting, soon after my husband came over from Africa, I saw a notice with the words, 'Prayer and Praise' written large at the top. I couldn't read any more as I'm as blind as a bat without my glasses, but Prayer and Praise sounded just fine for me. I told my husband about it because, where we had been in Africa, we had never attended anything as big as the meetings I was discovering over here. I had gone over to Tunbridge Wells to a Prayer and Praise meeting and it had been so beautiful that I was eager to take my husband to a similar gathering. I had no idea this was to be a healing meeting.

'I shall never forget that evening. It was 11th October 1980. We joined up with Christian friends round the corner and, arriving in good time, found seats together down near the front. The hall began to fill up rapidly but beside us two seats remained empty. Of course the first thing that struck me was that the heating must be full on because it was hot – too hot for me. So, even before everyone had arrived I stripped off my jacket and was feeling decidedly uncomfortable and over heated. But people kept pouring in until the hall was packed – all except the two vacant seats beside us. Meanwhile, our friends from Africa, Joan Campbell and her husband Robin, arrived with their family. Normally, like most families, they would sit together, but that evening Joan and Robin spotted the two vacant seats near the front and told their family they would fill them and meet up afterwards. They had no idea they would be sitting alongside us. Again, it had to be God.

'At last the meeting began with a lovely time of worship and praise through scripture songs and it was only as time went on that we learned that the speaker was Ian Andrews and that he had a healing ministry. In no way had I come expecting a touch from God for my latent leukemia.

'Ian began by talking generally about healing, stressing the fact that God never changes and it is the church that has changed by no longer coming to God for healing in the way people came to him through Jesus Christ his Son when he was living on this earth. Ian also spoke about the different sensations people feel when God touches them for healing. He explained that some would feel a heat going through their body which might be as intense as a fire coursing through them. 'Don't move,' he told us, 'And don't go and get a drink of water. Just sit and let the heat burn through you and it will burn out whatever is wrong with you.' Sitting there listening I was so hot already that I couldn't conceive of any greater heat coming on me. But Ian then went on to say, 'If God thinks you are hot enough already he may send a cool breeze through you. You may become decidedly cold and wonder what is happening. Don't worry. God is freezing out the pain or growth or problem you have and bringing it to an end.' He went on to say that some people have neither of these sensations. For them it is as if they have touched a source of electric power and they begin to shake and tremble.

''But,' Ian told us, 'what ever happens to you, don't worry about it, don't look around at other people, but continue to look at Jesus. The moment you take your eyes off him everything ceases because God decides that all you are wanting is to see a few miracles instead of deeply identifying with his Son. So God leaves. And if God leaves this place and removes his Spirit nothing more can be done and people who would have been healed remain sick and go home disappointed.

''There is one other way God might heal you,' Ian continued, 'with no sensation at all. When the Holy Spirit is present, some of you will find that your pain or lump or paralysis or whatever has suddenly gone. That's the time to get excited because God has met your need. So,' Ian told us, 'let us concentrate on God and let him do his work as we look into his word to see the provision made for us.'

'But that was all I heard. God had already come by his Spirit because I keeled over on the floor with an anxious Joan Campbell once again bending over me, just as she had in the ambulance years earlier. 'You went the same colour as you did in the ambulance that day,' she told me afterwards and added, 'I didn't think you could give me a fright like that twice in a life time!' But I was sublimely oblivious to what was going on. Evidently there was quite a stir in the crowd as I went down but Ian told them not to worry, 'I don't think she has fainted,' he said. 'I believe it is the Spirit of God working in her.'

'When eventually I opened my eyes I was holding Joan's hands, but was experiencing a most extraordinary sensation. I could feel the blood rushing through my veins and arteries. That's the only way I can describe it. Seeing I was opening my eyes my dear friend whispered anxiously 'How do you feel?' and went and fetched a glass of water. But, praise God, I didn't need water.

'Getting up off the floor I sat on my seat and, it had happened. I was healed! God had sent his healing power throughout my entire body by my blood stream and I was healed! I hadn't the slightest doubt or hesitation. God had so simply done the impossible for me.

'The Lord has such a wonderful sense of humour. I hadn't known it was to be a healing meeting and I didn't even hear the teaching Ian gave to quicken our faith. In his mercy and love God had gone to work on me after only a short time in the service. By the time I had received my divine blood replacement it was almost the end of the service. With a heart full of joy and gratitude I joined the queue and went forward to thank God for his kindness and love toward me.

'The result of God's healing has been that I need to wear the extra sweater or cardigan like everyone else on a cold day; my need for 'air' is as normal as anyone else, but perhaps most noticeable of all is the fact that my energy since that night could almost be described as embarrassing! However, not wanting to be accused of a twisted imagination or told of an even more remarkable remission, I made an appointment and went along to see my doctor.

'As I entered his surgery he looked up at this example of robust health standing there. 'Well, Mrs Norton,' he began. 'What's wrong? What can I do for you?' I started by saying, 'I thought I ought to come and visit you,' and then went on to tell him what had taken place and that God had touched me and taken away every trace of leukemia. He listened quietly and then did a few tests which seemed to satisfy him, but to cover himself and make certain that the amazing claim I was making was really true, he sent me to the hospital. There I was subjected to all kinds of tests and had no worries at all about the outcome. Each and every test came back 100% OK. Only God can do such a thing and to him I give all the praise and my heartfelt and joyful thanks.'

I felt a total failure

Paul Feasey works in a food factory in the Midlands in England. He has a wife, Brenda, and a lovely family, and can look forward to a future that is in total contrast to the years of loneliness that lie behind.

'Right now! Settle down all of you and get out your reading books. I don't want to see any of you wasting time. Read to each other as you have done before and I will come round and listen to as many as I can. Hurry up! And don't let me hear any talking.'

Paul Feasey looked round the classroom before slowly getting out his copy of 'Peter and Jane'. Then he moved over to one of his thirty-one classmates doing remedial reading.

'O.K.,' he said, 'I'll listen to you. Get on with it.'

It sounded good and gave him a rare ego trip to act as teacher, but no one, not even the real teacher, was aware that he couldn't have read about 'Peter and Jane' if he had wanted to.

The boy beside him falteringly droned out the words in a boring monotone and Paul tried to look interested and confident. But inside his stomach was tied up in knots. Just suppose his 'pupil' ground to a halt over a word. What would he do? Paul could no more have helped him than flown because unknown to him or anyone else, he was acutely dyslexic.

School was a nightmare for Paul, a daily torture which he dreaded. He would have given anything to stay in the peace and happiness of his home where there were no raised voices and no arguments and above all no dreadful situations when he would be made to look and feel a fool and an imbecile.

The youngest of five children, Paul lived as an only one and received plenty of love and affection from his parents. But there were problems even at home. His father, a diabetic, lost a leg through gangrene and eventually died when Paul was only just into his teens. Because of his father's disablement Paul never became involved in sport of any kind, so with his secret problem over reading and writing, he became convinced he was a total failure.

There was that awful day when he found himself faced by an eleven plus exam paper. Glancing round the room he saw everyone else writing eagerly while he picked up his pencil and had the greatest struggle just to get his name on the top of the paper. The exam paper was hopeless – just a load of jumbled letters. The next day the news swept like wild fire round the school that 'Paul Feasey had only put his name on the paper,' 'Paul Feasey was an idiot,' 'Stupid Paul Feasey.' No one understood. No one apparently wanted to understand. No one stood up for Paul against the cruel teasing and bullying that followed. It was grim.

Moving on to secondary school the deception began again and Paul became adept at bluffing his way through difficult situations. By this time his father had died and his mother would occasionally buy Paul a comic as a treat. He would sit there staring at the pictures and trying to look as if he was reading. It was not until many years later that Paul told her he could not read or write.

At last school days came to an end and Paul thought his problems were over. But this was far from the truth.

'Mum, I've bought a motor bike', he announced one day. 'It will make it much easier to get to work.' On leaving school Paul had found a job in a local factory and one thing he wanted more than anything was a motor bike – so that he could be like his workmates and be accepted as one of them.

For weeks this desire grew and Paul would arrive home later and later as he talked bikes and thought bikes and gazed at the shining monsters down at the shop. All the while he was saving his wages and dreaming of the day he owned a bike of his very own.

At last, one Friday, he achieved his great ambition and arrived home with a brand new bike which he petted and polished and generally loved all weekend. Then came Monday morning and he trundled it into the road, flung his leg over the saddle, adjusted the throttle and was ready for the big moment. A thrill ran through him as he switched on the ignition and took a last loving look at this great symbol of manhood before with a kick, it roared into life. It went like a dream – until a sharp bend was coming up ahead of him and his brain told his hands to turn left. But nothing happened. Some awful blockage between his head and his hands stopped the message getting through. Tearing straight ahead, he cut right across the road and crash! It had happened before on other bikes but Paul couldn't believe it could happen again. But it did and he found himself in Casualty at the local hospital being cleaned up and plastered and sent home.

Limping in that morning, all scratches and plaster, there was nothing he could say. His mother, hearing a noise, came through and when she saw him, burst into tears.

'Promise me you'll never ride a bike again,' she begged. So that was the end of a lovely dream.

'It was while all this was going on in my life that my sister had a baby girl,' Paul tells us. 'And it was eventually through Barry, her dad, that our lives were to be changed. But we didn't know that at the time and I guess I wouldn't have believed it if anyone had told me. Lives didn't get changed as far as I was concerned. And if you had a problem like I had over this reading business then that was my bad luck and I'd just have to go on bluffing my way through life till I'd had my lot.

'There were times when it was just frustrating, like not being able to read titles and names on the T.V., but there were other times when it really was a crisis. When I considered myself an adult I left home and lived alone until I met Brenda and we thought we'd get married. I proposed and was accepted but then I had the terrible confession to make, 'By the way, I can't read or write.' But God was good to me even though I didn't know him then, because I found one of her relations had the same problem and so she took it O.K.

'At the factory I was pretty safe for a while but then, as the years passed I'd get questions shot at me like, 'How come you've been here that long and you're not a Chargehand?' It always came when there were people around, in the Canteen or as we were clocking on or off. And I'd have to deceive again by being big and laughingly passing it off with some remark like, 'You won't find me buckling down to the managers.' My life wouldn't have been worth living if I'd told the truth and simply said, 'I wouldn't dare become a supervisor because I couldn't fill up production sheets as I can't read or write.' Imagine the reaction that would bring. No, I got by through bluffing and deceiving and lying.

'One day I was sitting in a pub and a chap picked up a matchbox and read the funny on the back of it. Then he handed it to me. 'What do you think of that then?' Well, to me it was a white box with a load of blue blurs on it, but I took it, allowed what I thought was long enough to read the joke, gave a chuckle and handed it back. But he was going on about it so I had to pretend I needed the toilet and got up and left him.

'That was life, repeated in different situations over and over again and I thought that's how it would go on. But one day I met Barry and he started talking about God and Jesus and that he'd met Jesus through a chap he worked with. It seemed a bit odd to me but we kept meeting and he kept telling me more and saying he'd been saved. Eventually he told me this chap Ian Andrews was coming and would I go along with him to hear what was said. I went, not knowing what I expected. There was some singing and a prayer and then Ian Andrews stood up and started to tell his life story. I guess God knew it was just what I needed because it made a lot of sense to me. He told us he had stammered since he was four and the doctors kept saying it would soon go, but it didn't. At school the children had laughed at him and he felt out of it and insecure and unhappy – well, he could have been talking about me with my past. He went on to the problems he had over getting married when he couldn't say 'I will' or 'I do' without spluttering all over the place and how, although he said he didn't believe in God at the time, he had prayed and found God had done a miracle so he could speak clearly right through the wedding service.

'Later on he told us he came to believe in God and Jesus Christ again but he still had this terrible stammer. I remember he said he told God he didn't think it was fair that he had to stutter like that and God really brought him up sharp. God spoke to him somehow and said, 'You don't get what's fair. If you got what's fair then you'd go to hell because that would be fair. If you want, have your own way and have what is fair and go to hell, but if you want to come into My kingdom you must submit to the way I do things and you'll find it will be a blessing to you.' That shook him. But he went on that evening to tell us that the most unfair act that was ever perpetrated was the crucifixion of Jesus. He'd not done one single thing wrong and was totally righteous but God allowed his own Son to be killed so we wouldn't get what was fair but would receive God's love and favour. As I say, it all made sense to me, but being in my state I hoped I might get healed as I sat there! I think it was as Ian was describing the suffering of Jesus and the lashes he bore for our healing that I made up my mind to go and speak to him afterwards.

'That was amazing. I went up and admitted my problem and, before I knew what was happening Ian put a Bible in my hands and told me to read it. And I did! I couldn't believe it. Instead of scanning the letters backwards and seeing them in a jumble, they were all clear and orderly and, above all, they made sense.

'That was November 1980, the night my life began to turn around. I say began, because after that evening I went along to church regularly on a Sunday but lived as usual through the week. I continued to swear and smoke and carry on as before but at the same time tried to fight my way through to God in a sort of way. But as I went to church I picked up some of their songs and I found myself singing them at work and the next minute swearing. It took a while before it dawned on me that that wasn't right and then I found it was the swearing that stopped, not the singing.

'Eventually, on 20th January 1981 I persuaded Brenda to come with me to a prayer meeting at a housegroup. God had his hand in that because she couldn't see the point in all this church business. Anyway, she came and as soon as she went in I really felt God was there. We got talking about being saved and I had always thought God had to do everything but that night it was explained that it was up to us to respond to what God has already done for us through Jesus. That was a wonderful night because I wasn't the only one who broke down and invited Jesus into my life, Brenda did as well. We both became Christians that same night.

'Up till then I had felt so inferior I really couldn't live a full life. We had one little girl and that was to be it because I didn't know if my problem would be handed on to my children. But God has set me free and it's wonderful. He has shown me he wants the very best for me and that he loves me. He's taken away the cause of all my hopelessness and rejection and he has saved me and made me one of his own loved children. My desire now is to go straight ahead with him.'

God kept his hand on me

George Ray is an economist who has been working in a research institute for more than twenty years. He is also Visiting Professor of Economics at one of the English universities.

'I was born in Hungary into a middle-class Jewish family. We were not orthodox Jews but religious in the liberal sense in that we observed the great holidays – New Year and the Day of Atonement. That was as far as religion went in the family. Life was pleasant and as a young man I started my career with a big industrial concern expecting to work my way up in the company and make a good job of life. But I had not reached my mid-twenties when the Second World War broke out and everyone's plans were upset.

'As in many European countries the young men were called up and I could be no different to the others of my age, but as a Jew, of course I was different in that I was sent to a labour camp rather than into the regular armed forces. For today's people it is difficult to imagine what one of those labour camps was like. I was sent to Transylvania to help build a railway line and the contrast between home and the business world and the conditions in camp was almost indescribable. There were two hundred of us crammed in a barracks which allowed only enough space for each man to lie down. We were so close that it was impossible to turn over unless those on either side turned with you. Any barracks that can take two hundred men, even in cramped conditions, is a big place but it was winter and to provide any warmth at all there was one small stove. We had to work on the railway line all day and then collect any waste wood we could find to feed that small stove. We slept on the floor and you only had a blanket if you had brought one with you. Even worse than the sleeping conditions was the lack of washing and toilet facilities. There was only one tap for all two hundred of us so to wash yourself was a difficult problem, not to speak of washing your clothes. On the rare occasions when I was able to wash a shirt and hang it out to dry I found it frozen solid in the bitter cold.

'Having finished this job we were sent home until the next call up. I used this breathing time to settle an entirely different aspect of my life. I had been in love with a girl for some two years and we decided to get married. How right we were! Six days after our wedding I was called up again.

'This time – it was in the spring of 1943 – I was sent to a building site in a small provincial town called Vàc, to work on the extension of a spinning factory which was supplying the German army. There was not one builder in that labour camp but we were very cheap labour and that was what mattered. So there we were, a lot of unskilled men erecting scaffolding and trying to make a reasonable job of the building.

'One morning I climbed up to the second floor and was standing on the scaffolding, high up in the air, thinking this was just another day. But it was a day that changed my life. Either the scaffolding was too weak or it had not been erected properly because suddenly the whole thing collapsed, sending me flying through the air. I do not remember what happened next but evidently I fell onto a bale of cotton on my back. That may sound a nice soft place to land, but a ton of cotton squeezed together and banded with steel strips is very hard. The next thing I knew I was being bumped along a poor road in an ambulance and something in my back was very, very painful.

'There was a doctor in the ambulance and he kept pricking my legs and feet. 'Do you feel it?' he asked me when I was still only semi-conscious. I did. He then tried elsewhere: 'You still feel it?' and 'Do you really feel that?' When he repeated the pricks over and over I began to think he expected me to react differently, as if paralysed. Thank God, I was not. Then I lost consciousness again.

'Events in the coming months, from March 1943 onwards, were of utmost importance to our later life. I will let my wife take over now to report about what followed, which in any case stemmed from her direct experience.'

'The news of George's accident reached me by telephone. I was not at home, and the news came to my mother first who called me saying that George had had an accident and was in hospital. She broke the news as gently as she could but added, 'Do hurry, my dear.' I was obviously shaken. When I arrived at the hospital and was shown into the room where George lay he smiled weakly at me and said, 'It will be OK'. Only later did I learn that he only came round a couple of minutes before I entered the room. He was in agony day in, day out. Apart from inspection once a day no nurse came into the room where the Jewish boys were kept, separate from army patients. The young men helped one another out with bedpans and so on as best they were able to. George was not alone in his bed either. As a rule two were sharing a bed, as only the four beds in that room were allocated to Jewish 'labour campers'. But when the X-rays showed that George had broken two vertebrae he was then given a bed on his own. Even in the X-ray department he overheard the radiologist (a brother of one of the most notorious Hungarian Nazis) saying, 'Now that is enough, we won't take any more pictures of this case. A Jew is not worth the films that are so costly nowadays', – as if George were but a lifeless object and what was told in his presence did not matter at all.

'No treatment followed those X-rays for the next two weeks. This was more than my father could bear. There he was with all the means and yet his son-in-law must suffer ill-treatment – and no treatment medically – in this military hospital. Did we have to witness this without any possibility of helping? After a while my father did find a way. By making discreet enquiries he found out who was the consultant visiting the hospital for orthopaedic cases. Then he went to see this surgeon privately, offered him a considerable sum of money and they plotted together how this doctor might, by 'mere coincidence', enter the Jewish room, otherwise out of bounds for him, and find a case that was interesting for the sake of his research. He could then ask for permission to treat it.

'So that is what happened. The snag was that by then the vertebrae had started to grow together in the wrong way. Before setting the spine into plaster properly the bones had to be rebroken and stretched into the normal position. This was done by hanging George up horizontally by his hands and feet, and allowing the spine to curve and the wrongly grown pieces to break, thus forcing them back into their normal place by the sheer weight of the body. He fainted several times under the pain because this treatment was done without any anaesthetic. Finally it was over and he was put in a plaster cast that started at his neck and ended at the hipbones, all around his body. With this plaster on at least he was mobile and not bedridden any more.

'The way he stood up to all this suffering and humiliation was something I never understood. There was no complaining, just encouraging words for me that all would be well. He was in that hospital for six months altogether. With his plaster on he was able to help the other bedridden patients and also to keep the hospital rule to carry his own bedframe once a week down to the hospital yard where it was 'disinfected'. This meant flaming through the iron frame and mesh to kill the bedbugs hidden there. Yes – bedbugs were everywhere, they crawled on the wall, crept under the plaster and were biting continually. The only relief came from the long knitting needles George used for scratching himself. According to him this was perhaps the most irritating thing he had to endure.

'One day while all this was going on an extraordinary person visited our home. It was not just a casual encounter, but one that had the greatest significance not only to my life but to that of many others as a consequence. And this is what happened.

'The firm that supplied my furniture sent along a woman whom they recommended as a specialist in making loose covers. I needed them for protecting the upholstery in summertime (as was customary in Hungary). She was a foreign lady, Polish, but we were able to converse in German. While she was busily cutting the material she started chatting. 'You are Jewish, I believe?' I was taken aback by this bluntness. 'You have a lovely flat,' she commented and then carried on, 'A great collection of books, too. Do you have a Bible?' This I found even more bizarre. After all, religious matters are really private: this woman is a bit too inquisitive, I thought. 'No, as a matter of fact I have none,' I answered, wishing to put an end to the conversation. Still she carried on. 'Do you have at least an Old Testament that you read and know?' 'No, neither,' I admitted becoming somewhat embarrassed. 'Oh, that is so sad,' she commented with real sincerity in her voice, 'A daughter of Zion and yet she does not know her own Scriptures.' Daughter of Zion? What an odd but lovely way to describe a Jewess, I thought. I had never heard this expression before. She continued with a few more probing questions, then she put down her work and started to speak to me about herself.

'She was a Gentile but married a Jew in Poland, and now she was sharing the fate of her Jewish husband as a refugee after Hitler's occupation of Poland. She told me how the orthodox Jewish family mourned the 'lost son' at the time of their wedding because he married a girl outside his religion, yet how both of them were happy and united in their faith in Jesus, the Messiah of the Jews. How later, when her mother-in-law fell ill she asked them to her bedside before she died and wanted to hear about this Jesus, and then died in peace believing that he really was the Son of God who forgave her sins.

'The whole concept was totally alien to me. Would you believe that it was possible to live among Christians, in a so-called Christian country and never be approached by anybody with such words? But it was. Never before, either at school or by any Gentile friend, and we had many, was I personally approached in such a way. Nor was George. True, I read many books in which, usually as a sideline, Christianity was mentioned, and even a few where the main theme was religious, yet it never occurred to me to take it as 'the' truth. It seemed to me a beautiful myth that I enjoyed reading as good literature. And now this woman, a total stranger, was telling me about matters she obviously believed in and presenting them with an authority, as if she not only believed in those things but knew them to be true.

'After her own life story she also spoke of life after death. That what we see here is just part of the world, and around us are unseen forces that we can only perceive if tuned in to God. She pointed out how God loves His children and is yearning for their company, and that all the evil on this earth does not come from God but is the result of sin committed by men seduced by a rebellious, anti-God, fallen angel. All this she presented as fact and I listened attentively but incredulously, yet, from that time onward, in the coming weeks and months life started to have some meaning, even some perspective.

'She finished her work and left me with a friendly look. I have never seen her again. Her name was Mrs Schaffer. Most likely she disappeared in one of the concentration camps – or gas chambers? – where Jews were taken when they were deported from Hungary by the German Nazis. I hope to see her in eternity and tell her about the fruit of the seeds she had sown.

'I would have forgotten this episode in the turmoil of our life in those days but it was meant to be otherwise. For some time it was my plan to take English lessons, and a good friend of mine recommended an English teacher but warned me that she was one of those 'believers'. That aroused my curiosity. And when we met, the rest was in the hands of Mary Hajos, my English teacher. She answered my questions in a new and interesting way, invited me to her house to meet her husband Emil, now a Christian but once an orthodox Jew who knew both the Old and the New Testaments well. They invited me to attend Bible studies held in their home and also in a Lutheran church. I became more and more interested but could not take for granted all the things I heard. I argued, debated, questioned everything but following their advice started to read the Bible to see for myself. Finally, it was neither Mary nor her husband, it was the written word that proved itself true to me. I read all the Gospels first, looked up references in the Old Testament, read the prophecies, and came to a point when I had to ask myself, can it be that Jesus, of whom the Gospels draw such a pure and perfect yet realistic portrait, was a dreamer, a madman or a false prophet? If none of them I must believe that what he said about himself was the truth. And did not one prophet after the other see – and describe in the distant future a Messiah like him? Is not Isaiah 53 a perfect description of Jesus and His ministry on earth?

'So it went on and on. Question after question – and the answers. Eventually I began to feel more or less convinced. Of course I would have loved to have shared all these major revelations with George but there was hardly any opportunity for this while he was in hospital because there we were never alone. But eventually the day came when, though still in his plaster, he was permitted to leave the hospital temporarily. For the very first time we could move into our little flat. His accident was in March, it was now November 1943. After having settled there I brought up the subject, carefully and cautiously, knowing that George was something of an agnostic and religious matters were outside his interest.

'However, I found him softer than I anticipated. 'I confess,' he said, 'that during many sleepless nights I often asked myself what life is about, why is there so much suffering and injustice in this world? Is there a God at all? If there is, does he care for mankind – or is everything happening without any order and planning, haphazardly and unpredictably? Yet when I considered my own case I felt that I could just as well have died or become a total invalid for life. Why was I granted more time to live? Was there anything I ought to learn first, or a human duty to perform?'

'When he shared these thoughts with me I ventured further and asked him to come along to a Bible study with me. He was hesitant. 'I tell you, my dear, I will come with you once for your sake and to show that I am not altogether agnostic to what you now seem to believe. However, if I find that this thing is not for me, and its whole philosophy is outside my way of thinking, promise me not to insist on my attending any such studies again; it would be a waste of time anyway.' I promised and we agreed.

'The occasion came soon. It was not unprepared. Mary and Emil – who only knew George from my account – prayed that the Holy Spirit would touch him during this first time. And so it was. Not that he said much about his impressions, he is not the type. But he came again next time without comment.'

'Let me now continue, after my wife's story. Once discharged from the hospital I had to return for physiotherapy two or three times a week for the next eight months but I was able to return to my job again. With my disability I was no use to the armed or unarmed forces. I could live at home and began to go with my wife to the Bible lessons with our new friends. It was not long before I understood what they were talking about and accepted the

Lord into my life.

'The next year, 1944, brought an entirely new situation. In March of that year the German army invaded Hungary and life changed dramatically for us once again. For no other reasons than being Jews, we were all sacked from our jobs, ordered to wear the yellow star and observe a curfew, and were only allowed to go in the streets at certain times. Next came the order to leave our homes and move into certain designated houses marked with the yellow star – a kind of ghetto scattered around in the city.

'The younger men soon began to disappear from these ghettoes, called up again for labour camps. So was I. In the beginning the steel corset I had to wear made some impression and I was sent home again. In the early autumn, however, posters appeared in the streets and in the ghetto houses ordering all Jewish men up to the age of sixty to report on the race course where there was no medical examination at all and therefore no excuse for me either. We were driven westward and once again I found myself separated from my wife, collecting sugar beet in the fields with a crowd of other Jewish men. But my family were busy back in Budapest. They heard that the Swedish and Swiss embassies were issuing passports to Jews – so-called 'protective passports' – and somehow managed to get one of these for me. But by then I was some fifty miles west of the capital. They knew my address, but the post could not be trusted, so how could they send it to me? Eventually, by making some discreet enquiries they found a man, a non-Jew, willing to find me and deliver the passport. I got it from the officer in charge who said that I could keep it in my pocket but that did not mean I could leave.

'So there I was, with a safe-conduct pass that was not accepted. I was not alone either because another man obtained a similar paper at the same time and found it just as ineffective. We knew that one day very soon we would be on the march again in the direction of Austria and we also guessed what the final destination might mean. The existence of the concentration camps was no secret any more although we could not even guess the full story of the Nazi operations at Auschwitz and elsewhere. In any case, the two of us decided to walk out and try to get back to Budapest. How crazy and risky it was we discovered only after the event, since in the camp we were cut off from the outside world and did not know that the Nazi hunt for Jews was by then in full swing. To cut a long story short we started walking on the highway with our rucksacks on our backs and the yellow star on our dirty, thinning coats, when the driver of an army truck offered us a lift in his tarpaulin-covered vehicle. He was obviously no great friend of the Nazi rule for when we mounted his truck we found another dozen young Jewish men in outfits similar to ours, also on the run. It was the driver this time, who was instrumental in saving our lives.

'Meanwhile my family had to leave the ghetto house. As the front came nearer and the Nazi grip strengthened there were to be no scattered ghettoes any more but one concentrated one that would make the Jews 'easier to manage'. Eventually, however I found my family at various places, partly in hiding. Those were very dark days and although we knew from the BBC news, which was faithfully listened to despite very heavy penalties, that the end of the war could not be very far away, the immediate prospects for survival were very dim indeed.

'It was at that time that Sweden and Switzerland, as neutral countries, tried another way to help. They particularly felt something should be done for those Jewish children who had either lost their parents or were separated from them so opened a few childrens' homes. One of them was organised by our friends, Mary the English teacher and her husband Emil, in conjunction with an established Jewish mission of the Protestant church. They needed adult helpers and we were pleased to join them. There were about a hundred and twenty children in the home, some of them with their mothers, and eight to ten adults as staff. The home started in November and in December the front came very near. By Christmas the Russian artillery was at one end of the wide street where the home was situated, and the German artillery was at the other end. We were in the middle, in the shelter of the deep cellar with all one hundred and twenty children. The noise was incredible, with gunfire and falling masonry, and we knew the house had been hit several times. In fact when the battle died down and the front advanced, my wife's parents came to see if we were alright but when they saw the rubble of the shattered home they turned and left, thinking that no one could have survived. Next day they returned, however, and venturing among the ruins discovered that we were trapped but everyone was alive. Once again, God had kept his hand on us.

'Of course, during the siege that lasted some two to three weeks, we had no food left and were starving. For weeks we had no water either but it was bitterly cold with heavy snow and the snow outside provided us with water. 'Liberation' came at last but not without some new difficulties that are better forgotten.

'Slowly life normalised after the destruction. I returned to my old job for a while. Then in 1948, Hungary became a communist country. My old company was nationalised together with most other companies and I became an employee of the state. Stalinist rule was heavy and rigorous. We continued meeting with Christian friends not only socially but for Bible studies and also went to church from time to time, but not regularly. Religion was not in favour and since almost everything was known by the party officials of that era we were in their bad books. We knew that they knew about us and every religious inclination, let alone going to church, was marked in our personal files. After the 1956 uprising, I got hold of my own personal file and saw the evidence of the thorough and detailed nature of that intelligence system.

'After the failure of the 1956 uprising in Hungary thousands of people took to the road trying to get out to the West. By then I was impatient to go. The idea of leaving our home country had been with us since about 1949 and my suggestion was that we should join the other 'walkers'. My wife, however, was more sensible. We had three children at that time, between seven and ten years old and she said, 'We should not undertake this with three children. If the Lord wants us out of here we will go out by train and in a sleeping car.' At the time this seemed totally hopeless but I gave up the idea of walking and we waited for God to act.

'He did. And she was right! The day came when the government started to issue passports. There were strict regulations prescribing who could ask for a passport without any promise that those in the right category would necessarily obtain one but one of the privileged categories was that of the registered disabled. I was one of those, thanks to my accident.

'So I got my passport and that took my whole family by train out of Hungary and eventually to England. Our first three months were spent in the guest house of the Hebrew Christian Alliance in Ramsgate where our children started to go to school and I began my job-hunting. Eventually I found one in London and, with the help of the Alliance and others, we were able to settle down in North London.

'All this was wonderful but I still had a health problem, stemming from my accident. Every few minutes I had to change position or the pain in my back started. In sedentary occupation this is not easy but manageable. However I had to attend conferences and meetings requiring sitting for longer periods. This was difficult indeed for me and I had to ask for medical advice. An operation might have been one possibility but no one wanted to take the risk of damaging any of the nerves near the spine as this could have left me paralysed. I was offered a variety of painkillers but one cannot live on painkillers. Swimming was good but brought only temporary relief and water treatment at Bath gave relief for a couple of months but eventually I was back in the usual situation. So I thought, 'Well, here I am with this backache, but there are many people in a worse condition and I must accept that I will be like this for the rest of my life.'

'In Hungary we had attended the Lutheran Church. From the time we arrived in England we became members of a Congregational Church which received us with love. Gradually we made friends there and felt quite at home. We attended church regularly and the children went to the Sunday school where they were enthusiastic members of the Cubs/Scouts and Brownies/Guides attached to the local church.

'When my daughter Julie was about twelve she started to rebel and told us that she found churchgoing stupid and opted out as best she could. We thought it better not to force the issue, so instead we prayed that she should find the Lord for herself. Then, when she was 13, we arranged a summer camping holiday for her with the Torchbearers at Capernwray Hall in Lancashire and she wrote to us from there that 'she had given her heart to the Lord'. In her case this was not a childish whim but a serious commitment. From this time onward she was like a torchbearer herself not only to the rest of the family but also to many others. She stirred us all up and when we reached the point of wanting to know more about the Lord and were longing for deeper experience it was she who found for us the Fellowship, not far from our home, where we have been worshipping for the last twelve years.

'When we first joined it was only a very small house-group but it has grown into a congregation of considerable size since then. But it was in the initial state of a housegroup when our leader invited Ian Andrews for a series of talks about healing. We had the usual time of praise and worship and then Ian began to speak. He took as his reading the first few verses of Leviticus 1, all about the burnt offering in the days of the Levitical priesthood. He told us that the burnt offering was the very first offering God wanted, an offering that was given wholly for him. He went on to quote from the third verse in the Authorised Version of the Bible which points out that this offering was given by the persons 'own voluntary free will'. Ian explained that God wanted above all that His people should of their own 'voluntary free will' offer themselves as living sacrifices to God; that they should give every part of themselves freely to God and make him their Lord irrevocably. Then to those who are willing to be burnt offerings in this manner God makes available his Holy Spirit, the same Spirit that filled Jesus. Ian led on to the wonderful fact that Jesus not only died for our sins but that 'by his stripes we have been healed' and this healing is freely available to those who accept and acknowledge his Lordship.

'To be frank, I was not even thinking of healing. After thirty years with my condition it had become normal to me. I simply accepted it. It was true that after a while, in almost any position, my back started to ache but I was quite reconciled to that. It was almost at the end of the meeting that somebody mentioned my case to Ian and he came to me to ask what was wrong with me. I told him and he asked me to sit down so that could look at the length of my two legs. He found one a little longer than the other and I told him that that might be so though I had never noticed it.

'Ian's answer was remarkable: 'George', he said, 'I don't know whether your pains come from the uneven length of your legs or from the old fracture. But one thing I know, that God loves you and says to you today that you have suffered enough. I believe he wants to heal you here and now. Let me pray for you.'

'It was a long prayer and all I could feel was intensive heat going through my body. It passed through my mind that if God really wanted to heal me I would accept it with pleasure – but I was still in doubt. So for the next few days I paid particular attention to my condition and I realised that those severe pains did not come back. Weeks passed, a few months passed and I was still free of symptoms. From that time, though sometimes my back is stiff and I need a walk to loosen it up, there is a tremendous difference. The severe pain I used to suffer has never returned, thank God.

'The damage to my spine was an extremely painful affair but it greatly contributed to my accepting Christ and it directly led to my coming to England. Without that accident I certainly could have – and probably would have – ended up either frozen to death on the Russian front or gassed in one of the Nazi concentration camps, as so many of my contemporaries did. It was God's love that permitted my accident to happen and it was the same love that put an end to its painful consequences in his chosen time.'

Conclusion

It is with great joy that we can publish this book and tell the Good News that Jesus wants you well. With a medical service under such pressure and long waiting lists for treatment, we need an alternative answer. Take heart, there is one.

It never was God's intention that man should suffer from sickness or disease in any form. Jesus came to bring us an abundant life. He said, 'I am come that they may have life, and have it to the full' (John 10.10).

How could a loving God want people to suffer?

Is God sick? Is there and can there be any sickness in heaven?

If there were, heaven would be far from perfect! – No! God's will is health. Even Jesus taught people how to pray – Thy *will* be done on earth as it is in heaven (Matthew 6.10).

God created man and woman to enjoy perfect health and happiness. Everything was blessed and Adam and Eve had all they needed. They talked and walked with God and there was no fear, only love. Unfortunately, this did not last long before Satan with his wiles tempted them to disobey God. Adam and Eve ate of the tree God forbade them to eat of. Eve first, followed by Adam. 'And the Lord God commanded the man saying, 'You may freely eat of every tree of the garden, except the tree of the knowledge of good and evil, and of blessing and calamity, you shall not eat, for in the day that you eat of it you shall surely die'' (Genesis 2.16,17). 'And when the woman saw that the tree was good, and that it was delightful to look at and a tree to be desired to make one wise, she took of its fruit and ate; and she gave some also to her husband and he ate'

(Genesis 3.6). Immediately after that, Adam and Eve lost their relationship with God, walking away from his provision for them, which was freedom from fear, sin and sickness. They had not known what pain was, or felt arthritis, stress or anxiety. They just enjoyed heaven upon earth, as God intended them to, but they chose to give away their birthright. Death would never have come had they not chosen to go their own way, as they were immortal up to this point. After this, Adam's sinful nature was inherited by all born after him. 'For because of union of nature in Adam all people die, so also by virtue of their union of nature shall all in Christ be made alive' (I Corinthians 15.22). Man's life span became progressively shorter as time went on. Death became his enemy and Satan was legally entitled to attack man in the form of disease and death. The results of sin were spiritual and physical death, unhappiness, sickness, disease, and the most awful thing they could have experienced – separation from a loving God.

As you trace through the Old Testament, you can see that God, whose nature never changes ('I am the Lord, I do not change' Malachi 3.6) wanted to show his mercy and remedy to man when he became sick. 'The Lord sent fiery serpents among the people and they bit the people and many Israelites died. And the Lord said to Moses, make a fiery serpent of bronze and set it on a pole, and if a serpent had bitten any man, when he looked to the bronze serpent on the pole with a steady expectant and continuing gaze, he lived' (Numbers 21.6-9).

The message was simple – look at God's remedy – the cross (serpent and pole). Everyone who did so and took the Lord as his healer found it worked. Imagine the thousands of the children of Israel, whole families, young people, babies, grannies, who had to leave Egypt to flee from the wrath of Pharoah, putting blood on their doorposts and eating their roast lamb in a hurry – their last meal maybe for a while (Exodus 12). This again is God's remedy for us shining through. The blood represented Jesus' blood being shed at the cross and the lamb they ate represented his body, beaten for us so that we could be healed. Christ is our Passover.

Death touched those firstborn in Egypt that night, but it didn't have any power over God's people. As they ate the lamb it became their health and strength. We read in Psalm 105.37 that there was not one feeble or sick person amongst their tribes. That's unusual to say the least, especially as they had been slaves for many years, probably deprived of today's health foods!

So we can see God's provision was always health, not sickness. But because of man's now-fallen nature, his body was subject to disease and there was as yet no permanent cure. Some individuals trusting in God were healed. As the Israelites believed Moses as representing God, they too were healed. But they were never free from the curse or power of sickness and disease. They needed someone, a man, to set them free.

So God set his master plan in action. It had been in his heart to do this long ago. He asked his son, Jesus, to leave heaven, to come to this earth and be born as a man. He looked no different from you or I, even though he was a King. He laid aside his divinity to represent us and perfectly do his Father's will on this earth. He did all that and was persecuted for it! Even as a young man, he knew he was God's son and could have wielded great authority if he chose to do so, but even he was subject to his earthly parents (Luke 2.51).

It wasn't until he was thirty years old that his divinity really began to show when God anointed him with the Holy Ghost and power so that everyone would know who he was and why he was here. 'This is my son, my beloved in whom I delight' (Mark 15.15). After Jesus had his Father's blessing, he began to demonstrate what God wanted to do for the fallen man. Jesus began to heal the sick, sight was restored to the blind, the deaf heard, epileptics were healed, lepers cleansed, the lame walked, paralyzed people got up from their beds and even the dead were raised back to life. This actually happened! Jesus was the answer. Here was God's will – healing, health, joy. Satan was having to deal with God on God's terms. Even though man didn't deserve it, God so loved the world that he gave Jesus. If it were God's will now for man to be sick, Jesus would never have gone against his Father's wishes and healed them. He healed *all* who came to him with their sick bodies.

Many were grateful and followed Jesus and worshipped him, calling him Lord, others just had their needs met and went their way, but he healed them *all*. Friends took their sick to Jesus (Mark 2.1-12) and there was great rejoicing when a demon-possessed man was totally given back his right mind (Mark 5.1-20).

Who is this man? What kind of a man is he?

This man Jesus is God's own son, anointed by his Father, who went about doing good and healing *all* who were oppressed by the devil. *All* must include you!

He hasn't changed and still wants to heal *you* and make you whole, mentally, physically, emotionally and spiritually. *We* have no special healing powers but we believe in Jesus who was wounded for our transgressions and with the stripes that wounded him we are healed (Isaiah 53.5). The beatings he took on his back were so that you can be healed and at the cross he took your place so that *you* can be free of all oppression and live in health and victory. Look at Jesus and what he has done for you, and as you do, thank him for suffering for you. He can touch you just where you are. He wants you to know his love and power in your life.

Some questions we ask . . .

I AM NOT GOOD ENOUGH – no, but Jesus is and he died for you and made you acceptable to him (John 6.37).

THERE ARE OTHERS MORE NEEDY THAN I – true maybe, but God has plenty for everyone and wants to do it for you. He fed over five thousand people at one sitting.

I'VE TRIED BEFORE AND IT HASN'T WORKED – *discouragement*. Forget the past! You can only live now, even Jesus prayed twice for some people (Mark 8.25).

GOD DOESN'T ANSWER MY PRAYERS – He does but he wants you to receive the answers. Don't give up and don't listen to doubt – God hasn't changed his mind about you. Be like the woman who pressed through the crowd to touch Jesus (Luke 8.43-48).

HE CAN LOVE EVERYONE ELSE BUT I DON'T KNOW ABOUT ME – *rejection*. He loves you as much as everyone else – in fact as much as his own son, Jesus (John 17.23).

I FEEL A FAILURE – you may *feel* a failure and have had failures in your life but God does not keep judging you. This does not stop you receiving God's blessings. He loves you, accepts you and can make you a new person. He doesn't heal you because of what you have or have not done, but because of what Jesus has already done for you (Romans 3.45).

MAYBE IT'S GOD'S TIME FOR ME TO DIE – God says he wants to give you long life (Psalm 91.16).

I CAN BE A BLESSING THROUGH SUFFERING – Jesus has already suffered in your place and does not want you to suffer any more. If God is satisfied with his son's sacrifice, then it is sufficient (Isaiah 53.11).

I AM SICK BECAUSE OF SOME SIN IN MY LIFE – this happened to a blind man in the Bible (John 9.2,3). It was common reasoning to believe you had a sickness because of some sin or wrong way of living. This of course does not help but Jesus demonstrated he was the answer to this when the religious Pharisees asked 'Who sinned?'. Also, the same situation arises with the paralytic man (Matthew 9.2). So the first thing Jesus said was 'Cheer up, your sins are forgiven, get up and walk!' He has forgiven you and he healed you when he died for you on the cross. But if you know you are living in a wrong way or have sins that get you down, cheer up – you can be free and whole. Jesus doesn't leave out your heart and just heal your body. He wants to do both, because he wants you well.

I DON'T HAVE ENOUGH FAITH – God doesn't want you to strive to get faith. As you look to Jesus, he imparts his faith to you. This is illustrated by the man who asked Jesus to heal his deaf and dumb son (Mark 9.23-25). Jesus answered his questions for help by saying 'Why, all things are possible to him who believes!' At once, the father eagerly cried, 'Lord, I believe, help my weakness of faith,' and the boy was healed. How like us – Jesus even gave him the faith to believe and he can do that for you.